AF333442

LISTEN CLOSER

LISTEN CLOSER

Believing God's Truth Over the World's Lies

Brendt Blanks

PUBLISHED BY IRON HILL PRESS

Listen Closer: Believing God's Truth Over the World's Lies

Published by Iron Hill Press in the United States of America.

Library of Congress Cataloging-in-Publication Data is on file at the Library of Congress, Washington, DC.

ISBN: 9798991329125

Unless otherwise noted, Scripture quotations are from the ESV® Bible (The Holy Bible, English Standard Version®), copyright © 2001 by Crossway, a publishing ministry of Good News Publishers. Used by permission. All rights reserved.

Cover Design: Rachael Milner
Interior Design: Upper Air Creative

CONTENTS

INTRODUCTION

"But you, O Lord, are a shield about me, my glory, and the lifter of my head."
- Psalm 3:3

There's a lot of noise in the world today, isn't there? Voices telling us who we should be, how we should feel, and what we should think. Many of us can barely hear God's voice, who speaks hope and truth into our hearts.

Friend, I understand the noise that competes for our hearts and minds. As a former Marriage and Family Therapist (MFT), and as a woman who has been saved by Christ, I have spent years witnessing, both in others and in myself, how profoundly our thoughts shape our lives. I've also seen firsthand how God's Word alone brings true transformation.

It's been years, though, since I was a practicing therapist. These days, I run She Gave It A Go, a home décor lifestyle brand I founded in 2015 after a fascinating career journey (I'll talk about it later in the book). Today, instead of waking up to meet couples or families in my office, I wake up and spend my days crafting marketing strategies, writing blog posts, and decorating my home for photo shoots. I could not possibly love my job more than I do. But I still take every opportunity to use my former skills and training. Why? Because I will never not be excited about helping people grow and improve. I guess it's how God made me.

One of the most powerful concepts when I was practicing therapy was a framework called Cognitive Behavioral Therapy (CBT). It's a life-changing yet straightforward approach, one that drives the philosophy of this book, and one that, especially when paired with Scripture, can radically transform your life. What's it all about? Glad you asked.

CBT teaches that our thoughts shape our behaviors and feelings. Change begins not with forcing ourselves to "feel better" but by reframing how we think. And when our thoughts are based on the living Word of God, truth that never changes, real, lasting hope takes off. Paul understood this and powerfully communicated it in Romans 12:2: "Do not be conformed to this world, but be transformed by the renewal of your mind, that by testing you may discern what is the will of God, what is good and acceptable and perfect."

Hope kept me going as a therapist, pulled me through rough times, and empowers me daily to infuse my work with the Gospel so that others might come to know God. Hope is a powerful reality, one that is most perfectly realized in Jesus.

But the world can work to rob us of our hope. It's easy to get beaten down by the circumstances of life. And when we find ourselves down, sometimes it's hard to know the way out. Have you ever had someone tell you, "just move on," "stop worrying," or "be thankful"? Maybe they even encouraged you to "pray more." People usually have good intentions, but if it were as easy as flipping a switch to change our feelings, we would all do it without a second thought.

The truth is, lasting change doesn't come from simply trying harder. It comes from listening closer, leaning into God's Word, ignoring the messages we hear from the world (and sometimes from within ourselves), realigning our thoughts with His promises, and letting His truth reshape our lives.

Living with hope isn't about ignoring hard feelings or pretending everything is fine. It's about remembering that our true and living hope is Jesus Himself.

As you journey through these 31 days, you will likely find that your feelings begin to shift, not because you're forcing them to, but because you are renewing your mind daily with the Word of God. Scripture lays this foundation clearly. In Philippians 4:8, Paul says, "Finally, brothers, whatever is true, whatever is honorable, whatever is just, whatever is pure, whatever is lovely, whatever is commendable, if there is any excellence, if there is anything worthy of praise, think about these things." Our behaviors naturally shift when we focus our thoughts on what is true, noble, and good. Our feelings follow.

This is something I practice in my own life. And friend, let me tell you, it is a daily practice. It's like building a muscle. Over time, you get stronger. The more you train your mind to listen closer to His truth, the more you'll live in the peace and hope He promises.

The narratives we tell ourselves matter. Isaiah 55:8 reminds us, "For my thoughts are not your thoughts, neither are your ways my ways, declares the Lord." The world's voice will tell you, "you're not enough," "you'll never change," and "this is just the way it is." The only problem with this is that the world is a liar. On the other hand, God's Word says, "you are my beloved," "you are more than a conqueror," and "I have good plans for you." And God's Word is true. Always.

When you swap the worldly lies for God's truth, it changes everything. Your thoughts change. Your behaviors change. And, yes, your feelings change. The fear that once was crippling, loosens its grip. The discouragement that weighed you down begins to lift. Joy takes root. Hope rises. And it's not the fleeting kind of hope that the world offers. It's a living hope, anchored in the person of Jesus Christ.

Isaiah 55:12 declares, "For you shall go out in joy and be led forth in peace; the mountains and the hills before you shall break forth into singing, and all the trees of the field shall clap their hands." This devotional is here to help you take simple, daily steps into this kind of hope. Psalm 119:105 says, "Your word is a lamp to my feet and a light to my path." Each day of this little book offers you a way to pause, reflect, and realign your thoughts with the Word of God.

Imagine for a moment the woman you're becoming: the woman God is shaping through this journey.

She's not constantly weighed down by the relentless pressure of the world.

She knows how to catch anxious, fearful thoughts and replace them with God's truth.

She recognizes the lies that once held her captive and walks confidently in His promises.

She has unlearned the world's story about who she is and embraced God's story instead.

She doesn't pretend hard things aren't real, but she refuses to believe that hard things get the final word.

Her heart is steady. Her mind is at peace.

Joy marks her life, not because every day is easy, but because she listens closer to God's voice that never fails.

That's where you're headed, dear friend. And it all begins right here, right now.

You don't have to muster up the strength to become this woman. You just have to show up each day, willing to listen. Willing to swap the old, worn-out thoughts for the life-giving truth of God's Word. Willing to trust that God's thoughts about you are better than anything the world could ever offer.

Each day's devotional will challenge you to reflect on your thoughts and examples of the world's impact on you, reframe your thoughts by replacing worldly one-liners with the true words of Scripture and biblical teaching, and respond by considering practical steps to anchor your life in living out what you've read in God's Word that day.

Over the next few weeks, I encourage you, no, I beg you, to trade the world's noise for the steady, unchanging truth of Scripture. But, remember, this is not about achieving; it's about abiding. Abiding in His Word. Abiding in His love.

And one last thing: you're not alone. Every word in this devotional was prayerfully written with you in mind. I'm right here alongside you, cheering you on, praying that you'll encounter the God who sees you, knows you, and loves you beyond measure. I'm so honored to walk through these 31 days with you.

So, let's begin, friend.

Let's quiet the noise, lean into the Word, and listen closer to the one who lifts our heads and fills our hearts with hope.

Day 1
The world's lies tear you down.
God's truth builds you up.

For whatever was written in former days was written for our instruction, that through endurance and through the encouragement of the Scriptures we might have hope.

- ROMANS 15:4

It usually starts quietly: a comparison whispered while scrolling Instagram, a sigh in front of the mirror, a voice that doesn't sound like yours but somehow always knows exactly what to say to make you feel not enough.

"She's a better mom."

"You're the reason he's upset."

"You'll never be able to say that without losing the friendship."

"You're too much." Or maybe, "You're not enough."

Sound familiar? You're not alone.

The world is full of voices, but not all of them speak the truth. Many don't. And one of the voices that can be the hardest on us? Our own.

Those lies tend to ring the loudest when we're most vulnerable, tired, worn thin, or already questioning our worth. That's why we need the anchoring, life-giving truth of God's Word, not just as something we believe generally as Christians, but as something we cling to personally, as His beloved children.

That's what Paul is getting at in Romans 15:4. He's reminding the early church, many of whom were Gentile believers without deep roots in the Jewish Scriptures, that all of God's Word was written for them, too. And it was not only written to teach, correct, or train (though it does all of that) but also to encourage. That encouragement leads to something powerful: hope.

God's Word reframes everything. But we must be willing to listen to His voice above others. On days when the world feels loud or the lies feel convincing, Scripture helps us turn down the noise and turn up the truth. You know the moments I mean:

The room you walked into, and instantly felt underdressed or unqualified.

The conversation that stuck with you and left you convinced that you said the wrong thing.

The way your child's bad day made you feel like you were failing as a mom.

The belief that if he's not OK, then you aren't allowed to be either.

These aren't just random thoughts. They're strategies of the enemy. They are lies repeated often enough that we begin to take them as truth. But take heart, friend. The world's lies crumble in the light, and God's Word is light.

Psalm 119:105 reminds us, "Your word is a lamp to my feet and a light to my path." The Bible doesn't just expose the lie. It gently guides us out of the dark. The world may make us feel small, but it has no real power to define us. So, how do we fight back?

By replacing lies with truth.

By allowing God's Word to shape how we see Him and ourselves.

By trading feelings and falsehoods for forever truths.

When we do, we don't just survive the battle; we stand strong in it, not in our own strength, but in His. Today, let's quiet the world and tune in to God's voice. Let's speak His truth over every lie that tries to take root. Because the only words worth building a life on are the ones God has already spoken.

Friend, you don't have to believe everything you feel. You don't have to carry every heavy thought that knocks on your heart. And you don't have to listen to the world when God is already speaking something better.

Listen closer. The truth is louder than the lies.

APPLYING GOD'S TRUTH

1. What lies from the world, or even from your own thoughts, have been tearing you down lately? Write it down, then search Scripture to find one truth that directly counters that lie. How does God's truth reshape your perspective?

2. When the noise of comparison, insecurity, or shame gets loud, what habit or practice helps you re-center on God's voice? Consider adding a verse or phrase to your daily rhythm to help quiet the world and tune into God's encouragement.

A PRAYER FOR TODAY

Father, when the world tries to name me, I listen to you instead. Your Word is truth. It lights my way, lifts my heart, and reminds me who I am. Help me recognize the lies I've believed and replace them with the hope and encouragement you've already written over my life. Speak louder than the noise, Lord, and build me up with your unshakable truth. Amen.

Day 2
The world says success is measured by status and fame. God says He knows your name, and that's enough.

The sheep hear his voice, and he calls his own sheep by name and leads them out.

- JOHN 10:3

Our world has a lot to say about what makes someone important. Our culture elevates platform, numbers, influence, followers, resumes, and hustle. It tells us our value is found in how many people know our name, what we've achieved, how well we've performed, or what we've built with our lives. If you think about it, success, according to the world, is public. It's measurable and marketable.

What great news, friend, that Jesus tells a different story. In John 10, Jesus uses the tender imagery of a shepherd and his sheep to describe His relationship with those who belong to Him. He says, "The sheep hear his voice, and he calls his own sheep by name and leads them out."

Pause for a moment and take that in. Jesus, the Son of God, calls us by name. He calls you by name. In the ancient Near East, shepherding was an up-close, "get your hands dirty" kind of job. Shepherds lived with their flocks. They knew the personality and quirks of their sheep. So when Jesus uses this picture, He's not just being poetic but personal. His love isn't distant or vague. It's intimate. He doesn't just love a general population. He loves you! He knows your name. He calls it out and leads you with care.

This verse has comforted me more times than I can count, especially on the days when I feel like I need to prove something. If I'm being honest, this is one of those areas where I still wrestle. I've built a career I love, which brings great fulfillment. When I land a new brand partnership or have a strong day in sales, it gives me a sense of accomplishment. There's nothing wrong with celebrating that. But the trouble comes when my joy and peace start to ride the highs and lows of my performance.

You might not relate to my exact scenario, but maybe you've felt it, too. Maybe a successful day is getting your toddler down for a nap or finishing your to-do list without falling behind. Maybe it's securing that new account, getting the meal on the table before 7 p.m., or being praised for how "together" you look when you're quietly falling apart inside.

None of these things is wrong. Many of them are good. But they make terrible identities.

Because what happens when they don't go well? What happens when your numbers drop? When your inbox is empty? When the effort doesn't match the outcome? Or when someone else seems to be doing what you were hoping for? Suddenly, we feel unsteady. Maybe even unseen. That's why the truth of John 10:3 matters so deeply.

Jesus doesn't wait to get to know you until you've succeeded. He calls your name before you do a single thing for Him. He knows you in the silence. In the mess. In the unseen, unshared, un-celebrated corners of your life. And He loves you still.

Isaiah 49:16 adds amazing imagery to our understanding of this promise. God says, "Behold, I have engraved you on the palms of my hands." This isn't written in erasable ink. It's engraved. It's permanent. And when we see the Gospel clearly, we know just how true this is. Jesus stretched out His hands on the cross to secure your name in love.

If the world's definition of success were true, Jesus would never have gone to the cross. He would've built an empire and made a name for Himself on this earth. But instead, He laid down His life in humble surrender to redeem the rebellion in the people He created. That is love. That's the kind of love that knows your name.

So what do we do with this truth? We root our worth in eternal things. We resist the cultural current that says we have to earn our place. We preach to our own hearts when the algorithm dips or the recognition doesn't come. And we remind ourselves daily that being known by God is not just enough; it's everything.

I want to live like that's true. I want to raise my kids like that's true. I want to sleep at night without replaying every unfinished task or unmet expectation. Because my worth isn't up for debate; it's already settled at the cross. And if you've come to faith in Christ, yours is, too.

So, sweet friend, here's the gentle nudge: You are not behind. You're not forgotten. You're not too late or too small or too anything. You are known by name. And that is more than enough.

APPLYING GOD'S TRUTH

1. What's one area in your life where you're tempted to measure your worth by performance or recognition?

2. Remember a time when you felt "less than" by the world's standards. How would that moment look different if you believed God's knowledge of your name was enough?

3. Is there a person in your life who might need to be reminded that their value isn't based on what they produce? How can you encourage them this week?

A PRAYER FOR TODAY

God, thank you for knowing my name and for seeing me not as the world sees but as your beloved child. Forgive me for chasing success or identity in places that can't hold the weight of my soul. Teach me to rest in your presence. Remind me that your love isn't earned; it's given. Help me to trust that I am enough because you are enough. Quiet the voices that demand more, and let me hear your voice louder than all the rest. Amen.

Day 3
The world says relationships are about what you get. God says they're about selfless love.

Do nothing from selfish ambition or conceit, but in humility count others more significant than yourselves. Let each of you look not only to his own interests, but also to the interests of others.

- PHILIPPIANS 2:3-4

Relationships come in all shapes and sizes. At one end, you have those tried-and-true friends, the ones who'd drop everything for you at 2:00 AM, the ones who appreciate your humor, and those who've seen you at your best and worst but love you all the same. Then, there are acquaintances: the people you smile at when you bump into them at your children's schools or a coffee shop, but don't dive much deeper with. And then, there's everything in between.

I want to talk about that middle ground, those friendships that seem to flourish only when you offer something. I've had those relationships, too. You know the ones, where you get the sense they only reach out when they need something, and the moment you can't meet that need, they're a little quieter. Now, many of those are people whose company I have genuinely enjoyed. But the pattern is clear: it's a relationship built on transactions.

The world often encourages us to build our circles based on who can help us, who can benefit us, or who can open the next door. It's easy to fall into that mindset, especially when faced with a culture that values networking and personal gain. And you know what? That's human nature. But God calls us to look at relationships differently. Instead of seeking what we can gain, He invites us to focus on how to love, serve, and glorify Him through the people He places in our lives. Our relationships are about what we can give them and how we can reflect God's love in every connection. That's a radical view, isn't it?!

Paul's letter to the Philippians is one of my favorite books in the Bible. It's so full of truth! His words in Philippians 2 are some of the most practical and powerful in the New Testament. Near the beginning of chapter 2, he writes: "Do nothing from selfish ambition or conceit, but in humility count others more significant than yourselves. Let each of you look not only to his own interests, but also to the interests of others" (Philippians 2:3–4). That is the recipe for friendships that glorify God.

Our friendships and relationships should never be based on what someone can do for us or how they make us feel. Instead, they should be about honoring others and putting their needs before ours, serving them out of love. And when we do this, we're embracing the heart of Jesus. In Philippians 2:5–8, Paul encourages us to have the same attitude as Christ:

> Have this mind among yourselves, which is yours in Christ Jesus, who, though he was in the form of God, did not count equality with God a thing to be grasped, but emptied himself, by taking the form of a servant, being born in the likeness of men. And being found in human form, he humbled himself by becoming obedient to the point of death, even death on a cross.

When we serve others with a humble heart, we model Jesus. We align our mindset with His, who showed the ultimate humility by giving His life for us. Our humility might look different, but it can still lead us to sacrifice, whether that's our time, energy, or resources.

Serving others isn't always easy. It can feel risky, and the fear of being taken advantage of is real. But we can't let that stop us from loving and serving those God has placed in our lives. By doing so, we reflect Christ, and who knows? Our Christ-like love may just be what draws them closer to Him.

APPLYING GOD'S TRUTH

1. Serving others is a great way to take the focus away from ourselves and reflect God to those around us. What are three ways you can serve others today?

2. In what relationships are you tempted to focus more on what you receive than what you give? How might God be calling you to shift your perspective?

3. What specific way can you practice selfless love this week, even when inconvenient or unnoticed?

A PRAYER FOR TODAY

*Lord, help me love others as you have loved me: humbly, generously,
and without condition. Free me from the temptation to view relationships as transactions, and instead, fill me with a heart that seeks to
serve. Teach me to count others as more significant than myself, and
to reflect your selfless love in every connection. Amen.*

Day 4
The world says it's too hard.
God says that He goes before you.

When you pass through the waters, I will be with you; and through the rivers, they shall not overwhelm you; when you walk through fire you shall not be burned, and the flame shall not consume you. For I am the LORD your God, the Holy One of Israel, your Savior. I give Egypt as your ransom, Cush and Seba in exchange for you.

- ISAIAH 43:2-3

I want you to think of the hard seasons of your life. The seasons of loss. The seasons of doubt. The seasons of despair, or uncertainty, or confusion. When I think about difficult seasons, I remember the early 2000s. In the span of 18 months, I lost my brother-in-law and my grandfather, our middle child was born prematurely, and my mother suffered a massive heart attack that almost cost her life. This was such a devastating season of loss and trial for us. To top it off, we had just purchased a new home, and my husband was working full time and in graduate school, so there was so much stress on top of grief and loss. I look back and all I can remember is how overwhelmed we were. It felt like every day brought a new wave of trials.

Friend, I ask tenderly, what does your season look like? Maybe you lost a child or a spouse, got a cancer diagnosis, or saw a relationship come to an end. Do you remember the moments when you felt like it was too much? When the waves crashed around you and you struggled to stay above water?

I have always wondered what it would be like to go through seasons of trial without our faith. When I lost my father to cancer, I was thankful for my husband, my children, my mother, and my siblings. It was critical to have them to lean on. But the Lord was my Rock. God was there when the grief threatened to swallow me.

When we face trials without a Heavenly Father to see us through them, they can and may overcome us. But with God to see us through, no trial is too great.

I have always loved the imagery of Isaiah 43:2–3. I love that it says, "when" you pass through the waters, not "if." The waters will rise. The storms will come. And when they do? What does the Lord promise? "I will be with you; and through the rivers, they shall not overwhelm you." Friends, that is what we call a promise. And every single one of God's promises is fully and completely kept. Though the trials come, they will not consume us.

God has always guided His people. Like the pillar of smoke by day and fire by night for the Israelites, God goes before us through challenges.

One of the reasons we feel so distraught in seasons of trial is that we don't know the outcome. We don't know where it will take us. I was driving through Atlanta not too long ago, relying on Google Maps to navigate as always. As you know, this can be a nerve-wracking exercise, especially on the busy interstates of a big city.

As I followed Google to the best of my ability, I realized I was on a special express lane reserved for "Peach Pass" members only. The catch? I was not a Peach Pass member. Before long, the lane turned into a dedicated road where I could not exit. Initially, I trusted Google to lead me correctly, hoping it was just a temporary detour. But as I continued, I started to become anxious. I was barreling along this road I knew I wasn't supposed to be on. I could look down and see the main Interstate. I noticed that the cars were moving much slower than I was. I knew I wasn't in the right place, but there was no way to get off. I was literally in a single-lane overpass above the main Interstate. Of course, I feared getting pulled over for not being where I was supposed to be.

The uncertainty of what would happen next really weighed on me. I don't know about you, but being pulled over is one of my least favorite things, and I could feel it coming. Eventually, I could exit the lane and return to the normal traffic flow. I didn't get pulled over that day, but sure enough, a few weeks later, a ticket showed up in the mail. As it turned out, I wasn't supposed to be on that road in the first place. It was one of those moments where I tried to avoid the consequences, but they still caught up with me.

Our lives often feel uncertain, don't they? We panic when in a tight spot because we don't know what's next. We don't know when we will be able to get off the road. We don't know what is around the bend. We don't know when we will be through the season of uncertainty.

But God promises to go before us. Even when it feels uncomfortable or scary, He's already there, paving the way. So when we stop to think about it, there really is no uncertainty at all. God is sovereign. He is in control. And His promises are true. The voice in our heads that says it's too much is our sin nature speaking. The truth is that no matter what you're going through, God has already seen you through it. His promises are sure.

APPLYING GOD'S TRUTH

1. What is one difficult season in your life where you clearly saw God's presence sustaining you?

2. How does the promise in Isaiah 43:2-3 change how you view current or future challenges?

3. List three ways to trust God more fully right now, knowing He goes before you.

A PRAYER FOR TODAY

Father, thank you for being with me in every storm and going before me in every trial. When I feel overwhelmed, remind me that you are my Savior, steady and sure. Help me trust your promises when the waters rise and the fire comes. You are my refuge, and with you, I am never alone. Amen.

Day 5
The world says beauty is a physical standard.
God says real beauty comes from within.

Friend, we can all relate to the pressure the world places on us regarding beauty. It almost feels silly to point out, doesn't it? But let's be honest, who hasn't wrestled with the standard of beauty that gets pushed on us? If you've never struggled with it, consider yourself incredibly blessed. Most of us have been there, me included.

I feel the pressure to look "put together," especially when doing something involving a camera, such as interviews or filming for my social media. Should I dwell on how others see me? Ideally, no. But do I? I'll admit, I do. Maybe not as much as some, but I think it's something many of us can relate to. Like many women, I often want to project my best, most polished version.

It's easy to get caught up in trying to meet external expectations. How wonderful it is that God's value system is so radically different from the world's. It's important to remember that true beauty, the beauty that God sees, comes from within. With God, you are enough just as you are.

Raising daughters has kept this issue close to my heart. My husband, Andy, and I have spent years reminding our girls that outward beauty is not an accurate measure of who they are. It's fleeting, subjective, and in the grand scheme of things, it's not that important. Still, there have been times when they've struggled with it.

We all have a picture of what beauty looks like, don't we? But where does that idea come from? It's likely shaped by the culture around us. The world has a precise definition of beauty, and it's primarily based on outward appearance. It's a harsh reality to face, and one that doesn't serve us well in the long run.

There isn't even an ounce of God that connects true beauty or value with our physical appearance. Scripture declares repeatedly that God values our character over our appearance. Nowhere is this displayed more perfectly than in 1 Samuel 16:7.

Do you remember the story? God had sent the prophet Samuel to choose David to succeed Saul as king of Israel. Do you remember how that went? Samuel knew that the new king was one of Jesse's sons. So, he did what he thought he was supposed to do: He looked for the son who seemed, from the outside, to be most "kingly."

Samuel started with the oldest son, who was tall and handsome. Surely this was the king! Nope. God told Samuel, "Do not look on his appearance or on the height of his stature, because I have rejected him. For the Lord sees not as man sees: man looks on the outward appearance, but the Lord looks on the heart" (1 Samuel 16:7). Samuel would end up going through each of Jesse's sons looking for the king. It wasn't until David, the youngest, was brought to Samuel that he felt God telling him this was to be the next king.

Now, 1 Samuel 16:12 says that David was handsome. But that's not the point here. David was the youngest and the last person in line for any inheritance. David oversaw the sheep, which was a very lowly task. He was brought in from the field when Samuel first saw him. He was said to be "ruddy." He had been working. He was almost assuredly sweaty and dirty. And God said to Samuel, "This is our guy."

1 Samuel 16:7 is God telling us how His value system works. This is how it worked when God chose David. And let's not forget that Jesus, the promised Messiah, was predicted in the Old Testament to be humble in appearance: "For he grew up before him like a young plant, and like a root out of dry ground; he had no form or majesty that we should look at him, and no beauty that we should desire him" (Isaiah 53:2). And yet, the Father could not value the Son any more than He did! Guess what? When God looks at you and me, the same value system is still at work. God still values inner beauty over outer beauty.

Proverbs 31:30 says, "Charm is deceitful, and beauty is vain, but a woman who fears the Lord is to be praised." I had this demonstrated to me most wonderfully on a trip I took with my older sister a few years ago. It was so special to bring my sister, Aren, along on a work trip to North Carolina. It was our first time traveling together, just the two of us, in years (we're both in our 40s). We had the best time, laughing, recalling childhood memories, and catching up on each other's current lives.

I was a guest of a rug manufacturer throughout a multi-day tradeshow. There were dinners and little gatherings, along with some formal meetings. During our trip, I had the chance to witness the depth of beauty within my sister. In the Uber rides, she was warm and engaging with the drivers, asking about their lives and treating them with genuine kindness and respect. When she met the employees of the rug company I was there to visit, she showed interest and always had a smile. Her "inner glow," which shone beyond her physical beauty, was noteworthy.

She brought her Bible and kept it open in our room, reading from it occasionally and sharing meaningful scriptures. Her kindness, peace, and selflessness reflected her faith in God.

This concentrated time together was a tangible, practical way of reinforcing for me the biblical truth that inner beauty surpasses outward appearances. It's true that when you see it lived out, it's captivating, genuine, and unlike anything else. It is a stark reminder that God's ways are not the world's, and wonderfully so!

Today, change your inner narrative. God sees and knows your heart and is at work behind the scenes, transforming your heart into one that looks like His through the power of His Spirit! That's real, true beauty! And it's worth praising God for.

APPLYING GOD'S TRUTH

1. Like my example above, recall a time with someone whose inner beauty left a lasting impression on you: a friend, family member, co-worker, or stranger. Reflect on their qualities, such as kindness, compassion, or faith, that stood out.

2. What influences your definition of beauty the most, culture or Scripture? How can you shift your focus to what God values?

3. How can you cultivate inner beauty through kindness, humility, or time in God's Word this week?

A PRAYER FOR TODAY

Father, thank you for seeing past what the world sees and looking into my heart. Help me to value what you value: a gentle spirit, a faithful heart, and a life that reflects your love. Teach me to find my worth not in outward appearances, but in who I am in Christ. Shape me to radiate beauty that honors you.

Day 6
The world says live for today.
God says your forever is already in His hands.

Blessed be the God and Father of our Lord Jesus Christ! According to his great mercy, he has caused us to be born again to a living hope through the resurrection of Jesus Christ from the dead, to an inheritance that is imperishable, undefiled, and unfading, kept in heaven for you, who by God's power are being guarded through faith for a salvation ready to be revealed in the last time.

- 1 PETER 1:3-5

I remember when the phrase "You only live once" first started popping up everywhere. It was the go-to excuse for everything, from splurging on something out of budget to making choices that maybe weren't the wisest. While YOLO has faded a bit as a fad, the mindset behind it is still everywhere. The idea is that today is all that matters, that we should grab what we can while we can. But deep down, even those who don't have a relationship with Jesus know there is so much more to life.

So many people around us live as if today is all there is. And when that's their belief, it shapes everything. Have you ever known someone who is just overwhelmed by the brokenness around them? Or maybe someone on the other extreme who is determined to soak up every drop of pleasure they can? And then some focus only on themselves. If today is all there is, why not? I've known people like this, and it always breaks my heart. You watch as they always chase the next big thing, only to come up empty because none of it truly lasts.

And yet, our world reinforces this concept at every turn. We're encouraged to seize the day and make the most out of every moment. Movies, songs, and even our own experiences advance this narrative. And there is a positive aspect to it, right? We should make the most of every moment. We should never take any one of our days for granted. There is too much Kingdom work to do, too much of God's blessing to experience. Yet, living solely for the present is a pretty risky mantra and goes against God's Kingdom values.

The world says today is all there is. Thankfully, friend, God's Word says something different.

In 1 Peter, the Apostle Peter encourages believers facing persecution. These were new Christians whom the Roman Empire was persecuting for their faith. Peter encouraged them to persevere with hope, knowing that the tough times they were experiencing were only temporary. Peter knew that these Believers would ultimately experience the fullness of God's salvation when they joined with God in eternity. The trials of this life would be over. Their forever life with God would begin.

Peter wanted his audience to stay faithful and to see their lives in this world as temporary. They were "spiritual exiles awaiting their heavenly inheritance." With this as the background, Peter said to his brothers and sisters in Christ: "Blessed be the God and Father of our Lord Jesus Christ! According to his great mercy, he has caused us to be born again to a living hope through the resurrection of Jesus Christ from the dead, to an inheritance that is imperishable, undefiled, and unfading, kept in heaven for you, who by God's power are being guarded through faith for a salvation ready to be revealed in the last time" (1 Peter 1:3–5).

What an incredible promise for today! The world is not the end of our story. We can know God's blessings on earth, and His goodness surrounds us. But we know that this world is fallen, and the effects of this are everywhere. If this world is all there is, it's no wonder some people are hopeless. But if you are in Christ, your fate is not to live only once. Your fate is a life after this one, a life Peter describes as "imperishable, undefiled, and unfading, kept in heaven for you." That is a future to hope for!

I attended a conference a couple of years ago where Beth Moore was speaking. I remember her saying something that stuck with me. She said that our focus should continually be moving upward toward heaven and downward toward Scripture. She kept repeating it over and over, driving home the point. She said this "upward and downward" mentality kept us focused on the truth of eternity and grounded in the wisdom of God's Word. I am paraphrasing her words, but I remember that visual so clearly. Upward toward heaven. Downward toward Scripture. And never looking to the world as our home.

Yes, sometimes eternity may feel distant and abstract. But our time on earth is fleeting. It's so important that we remember that this world is not our permanent home.

Friends, are you walking through your days with eternity in mind? As daughters of God, that's our inheritance: to live with a hope that reaches beyond today. So, let's slow down, soak in the moments, and remember what goodness lies ahead!

APPLYING GOD'S TRUTH

1. What does living with a "living hope" look like? How can we balance the call to be present today while keeping our eyes fixed on eternity?

2. How have you seen the "live for today" mindset shape the people around you? How might we lovingly invite others into a better hope?

3. Peter calls our inheritance "imperishable, undefiled, and unfading." What part of that description encourages you most in your current season?

A PRAYER FOR TODAY

Father, thank you for the mercy that has given us new birth into a living hope through the resurrection of Jesus. Help us to live not for the moment but for the eternal, fixing our eyes on you and walking in light of the glorious inheritance you've secured for us. Teach us to live with eternity in mind, and to find joy in the truth that this world is not our home. Amen.

Day 7
The world says improvement is up to you.
God says that growth starts with Him.

Therefore, if anyone is in Christ, he is a new creation. The old has passed away; behold, the new has come.

- 2 CORINTHIANS 5:17

The desire to improve is a good thing. If your motivation is pure, it can even be a godly thing. God only gives us one life on this earth, one body, and one mind. As much as it is up to us, we should steward these gifts as well as we can. Healthy habits can lead to a richer life, enjoying God's blessing and serving Him. Poor habits can inhibit our ability to get the most out of our lives and even limit our ability to serve the Lord. Self-help is good. But there is a problem with much of the self-help movement: you can only improve as far as you can take yourself.

We live in a world that's all about self-improvement, don't we? It sometimes feels like there's a never-ending stream of life hacks, beauty tips on social media, and articles telling us what we must eat to stop aging or lose weight. If we tried to follow it all, we'd never have time for anything else! It can be overwhelming to keep up, and it's tough to even know which trends are worth trying and which aren't!

The truth is, self-help only takes us so far. Our goals, whether sticking to a healthier eating plan, hitting fitness targets, or saving up for a dream home, depend on so many things: our willpower, our resources, and sometimes just life's little curveballs. And that's OK! We may be trying our best, and progress doesn't have to be perfect. Sometimes it's the little steps forward that matter the most.

Remember, it's OK to not have everything figured out right now.

Even those who can successfully achieve our self-improvement goals today might not be able to do so tomorrow. Just a few years ago, I was in a season of strong physical condition. I was at the gym five days a week doing CrossFit/ HIIT workouts that were awesome in their intensity. And then (as I mentioned earlier in this book), I injured my back. One surgery and years of physical therapy sessions later, my fitness goals have changed. Success for me is no longer burpees at the gym, but lifting a clothes hamper onto our bed.

The world can show us a picture of the "ideal you": prettier, faster, stronger, healthier, etc. It can feel like we must constantly work toward this version of ourselves. And can't we agree, how exhausting that is? But here's the beautiful truth: there's a kind of self-improvement that isn't dependent on us at all, and it's the most complete, whole transformation we could ever experience.

Isn't it comforting to know that God sees us just as we are and offers us growth that doesn't rely on our own strength or perfection? It's all about grace, the kind of change that truly lasts.

Take a moment and read 2 Corinthians 5:17, even if it's a familiar verse. The Apostle Paul wrote this during an epic chapter of his letter to the church in Corinth. Chapter 5, especially the second half, gives us a rich example of how God sees us and desires to use us to advance His Kingdom. Vs. 17 is the foundation for this usefulness and speaks directly to the heart of our "self-improvement" culture.

Here, the Holy Spirit speaks through Paul to share one of the most powerful truths about Gospel transformation. When we come to faith in Jesus, we are made new by the power of the Spirit. We are changed from a spiritually dead person to a spiritually alive person. But before we think this is self-improvement, we must look closer.

Paul doesn't say that when we come to faith in Jesus, God gets a wet-wipe out of His pantry and cleans off all the grime from our faces. He doesn't say that He runs a brush through our hair to make us more presentable. He doesn't give us a makeover or a mani/pedi. No, what happens is the moment we confess our belief in the person and work of Jesus, God, in His grace, puts us to death. That's right. He puts to death the old us that was a slave to sin and in the place of the old, dead us, He makes something new.

My husband, Andy, who is a writer and a preacher, has written this about the Gospel, specifically 2 Corinthians 5:17: "The Gospel isn't self-help. It's self-destruction." Those words ring so true! God does not create a better version of us. He puts to death the old you, and in its place gives rise to something completely new, something spotless and beautiful, a new life made, as Paul says in Ephesians 2:4, "after the likeness" of God.

God makes you perfectly new. And outside of the faith we confess in Jesus, this has nothing to do with us. In Christ, you are made perfect in God's eyes, regardless of your willpower, genetics, or discipline. In one way, it's anti-self-help, but in another, it's the ultimate self-help!

If it stopped there, it would be amazing. But it doesn't. God continues to remake us in His image through sanctification, the process of the Holy Spirit working within us to make us more Christ-like. As we grow closer to Him, we reflect Him more. This is so incredible that it's hard to process.

So you see, there is a life hack, if you will, readily available to you. It is the ultimate, comprehensive, holistic rejuvenation plan. And I have amazing news for you: it doesn't rely on your efforts! It starts with surrender. The rest is in God's hands.

APPLYING GOD'S TRUTH

1. How does knowing that you are a new creation in Christ change how you see yourself and your past mistakes?

2. How have you seen God transform areas of your life through sanctification? Identify specific instances where you have felt renewed or changed by His Spirit.

3. How can you continue to seek and embrace this ongoing sanctification process?

A PRAYER FOR TODAY

Father, thank you for making me new in Christ. In a world that pushes me to strive harder and do more in my own strength, remind me that true transformation begins and ends with you. I confess that I often lean on self-help when I should lean on your grace. Help me to surrender the parts of me that I keep trying to fix and instead allow your Spirit to do the work only you can do. Help me to become more like Christ, not through effort alone, but by abiding in you. In Jesus' name, Amen.

Day 8
The world says happiness is only found in success.
God says that joy flows from a grateful heart.

Yet I will rejoice in the LORD; I will take joy in the God of my salvation.

- HABAKKUK 3:18

Success can be fun, right? It's so wonderful to celebrate the start of a new relationship, a promotion at work for you or your spouse, one of your children's accomplishments, or something as simple as getting a compliment on an outfit you put together. It's normal to feel good when we succeed. But the issue is when we're conditioned to only feel good when we succeed.

The world rewards you when you are successful. Maybe as a child, you got a trophy when you won a game. As an adult, that reward looks a little different. Maybe you received a promotion because of what you had achieved for your company. Regardless of how young or old you are, we are conditioned to notice and strive for the rewards that success brings. Why? Because we're told that success equals joy.

The opposite can be true, too. If we don't occasionally get a "win," it's easy to get down. And what about when we compare ourselves to someone else's success? That kind of comparison can be a thief of joy.

I remember one time when I was surprised by a feeling that popped up inside me. It came out of nowhere! I was shopping and noticed a woman's cart was full of clothing. I looked in my cart and it had one shirt in it. And suddenly, I felt that this person was "better than me" because they had more in their cart than I did! I immediately realized this thought wasn't true, but my initial urge is fascinating. That was a feeling that was 100% influenced by the world. It's fascinating how we never know what messages we absorb from our surroundings. It's why it's so essential for us to ground ourselves in the truth of God's Word and not the untruths of the world.

How do we combat the world's value system that says, "Happiness is found in success"? By leaning into what God says about joy, something more lasting and less dependent on circumstances than happiness, and how we discover it.

I'm sure you've heard the saying, "Have an attitude of gratitude." I've told myself and my children this many times. But if our happiness only comes from success, we're missing what true gratitude is. Nothing brings out a grateful heart quite like walking through hard seasons (it's a paradox, isn't it?). True gratitude leads to real joy.

As I've mentioned, we've had some hard seasons. I watched cancer take my father. I've dealt with debilitating back pain, surgery, and lasting issues as a result. My son was in the ICU when he was an infant and almost didn't make it. These seasons, and others, will leave a mark on us, won't they? I know you've had your own seasons of trials, too. But, friend, trials have a way of opening our eyes to what we must be thankful for. Studies have shown this to be true; it's pretty much impossible to be feeling anxious when feeling grateful.

There is a moment in Habakkuk that records the prophet's dialogue with God as he wrestles with why God allows injustice and suffering to exist. But by the end of the book, Habakkuk comes to trust in God and His plan. He eventually professes his faith in God's justice and salvation even during uncertainty and hardship. How does this work?

Habakkuk 3:17–18 is a prayer that comes at the very end of the book, after he has wrestled with God's decision not to intervene or stop the bad things happening to His people. Hear the prophet's words: "Though the fig tree should not blossom, nor fruit be on the vines, the produce of the olive fail and the fields yield no food, the flock be cut off from the fold and there be no herd in the stalls, yet I will rejoice in the Lord; I will take joy in the God of my salvation." Wow! Israel had been taking the losses. Defeat after defeat. (And yes, it was of their own making, but can't the same be said for us sometimes?) And yet, in the end, Habakkuk could rejoice. This is the opposite of the culture we live in.

How do we do this? How do we rejoice during trials? There is something about being brought to our very hands and knees that enables us to see how much God is truly our all in all. It only happens by changing our narrative (sometimes over and over again) and listening closer to God's still, small voice. It's no longer saying things like, "I have so much to get done; I'll never get it all done today," to "I am grateful that God has given me a home to live in, and a fridge with food in it, and a sink to wash dishes in." It's flipping the negative statements we tell ourselves to a posture of gratitude.

In the excellent Disney movie, *Inside Out*, we see the emotions of the young girl, Riley, come to life as characters inside the "control center" of her brain. Recall that Joy is the primary emotion in charge of all of Riley's other feelings. I have always loved that Joy is the one who oversees all the other feelings. Remember what happens when Joy is pushed aside? Everything seems to spiral out of control. In the movie, Joy is the overarching emotion that keeps Riley's emotions in perspective. She wasn't the only emotion Riley felt, but the one that helped keep her on track.

Joy rooted in God's promises can never be taken from us. Success is exciting, but if our happiness depends on it, we miss the more profound joy of truly knowing Him.

APPLYING GOD'S TRUTH

1. How can you begin a daily habit of gratitude even when circumstances are difficult?

2. Think of a recent challenge or setback. What made it so challenging? Where were the blessings in it? Were you able to be grateful in the moment? Or do you need to express your gratitude to God now in hindsight?

3. If you don't journal already, I suggest starting a gratitude journal where you write down three things you're thankful for each day, even on challenging days. Reflect on how these blessings are signs of God's grace.

A PRAYER FOR TODAY

Father, help me to find true and lasting joy in you in a world that tells me joy comes from success. Teach me to cultivate a heart of gratitude, recognizing your goodness in every season, both in abundance and struggle. Let my joy be anchored in your promises, unshaken by circumstances, and a reflection of my trust in you. Amen.

Day 9
The world says fear change.
God says that change is the only way forward.

Behold, I am doing a new thing; now it springs forth, do you not perceive it?
I will make a way in the wilderness and rivers in the desert.

- ISAIAH 43:19

Let me be transparent for a moment. I don't always love change. It can feel unsettling. While I've gotten better at adapting to it over the years, my first instinct is often resistance. Maybe you've felt that too.

The world tells us to hold on tightly to what's familiar, to stay where it feels safe and predictable. Change, after all, brings uncertainty. And uncertainty is uncomfortable. Maybe you've heard the quiet voice of doubt saying, "You've built something good here. Don't risk it. What if the next step isn't as good?" I've been there. I've felt that fear creep in, especially when I sensed God was leading me toward something unfamiliar, while the world was whispering to stay put.

But friend, aren't we so thankful that God speaks a different word over us?

God tells us that change is often the doorway to what's next. He reminds us that to receive the new thing He's doing, we may have to relinquish what once was. And while that's not easy, it's good.

I remember standing at a significant crossroads. I had been working as a Marriage and Family Therapist, a career that felt like a calling. It was deeply meaningful and something I had studied for and poured myself into. My dad had been in the same field, so it also carried a sense of legacy. But when he was diagnosed with cancer, that emotional weight became very heavy. I found myself yearning for something that I didn't even know yet.

That unexpected "therapy" came through home decor. Yes, decorating! Re-arranging furniture, choosing paint colors, and creating cozy corners in our home brought me peace when life felt out of control.

I started posting photos of our home on Instagram, not to start anything big, but simply because I found it enjoyable. But God had more in mind. That creative outlet began to grow into an encouraging community. Women started reaching out, sharing how they felt inspired. One day, my husband looked at me and said, "What if this isn't just a hobby? What if this is God opening a new door?"

I hesitated. It felt scary to leave a career I had trained for. But the more I prayed, the more peace I felt, not in staying where I was, but in stepping into something new. And that's the thing about change: sometimes the peace we long for only comes when we take the step God asks us to take.

Eventually, I said yes to a brand-new path: full-time content creation and building a lifestyle brand that encourages women from the inside out. It was a big change, but it was God's next step for me. And I'm so grateful I didn't let fear keep me from saying yes.

So, friend, what change is in front of you right now? Maybe it's not career-related. Perhaps it looks like:

> A shift in your family dynamic

> A health diagnosis that has altered your everyday life

> A move you didn't plan

> A friendship or relationship that's shifting

A stirring in your heart that you can't explain, but you know something is changing

Whatever it is, hear this truth: God is not surprised by your change. Isaiah 43:19 says, "Behold, I am doing a new thing; now it springs forth, do you not perceive it? I will make a way in the wilderness and rivers in the desert." That isn't a suggestion, it's a promise. God is already working in your wilderness. He doesn't wait until everything is tidy to begin. He starts right in the middle of the unknown.

Maybe today your question isn't, "Will everything work out?" Maybe it's, "What is the next faithful step God is asking me to take?" And maybe, like me, you can begin by literally opening your hands. Sometimes when I pray, I hold my hands open as a sign of surrender. It's my way of saying, "God, I'm not clinging to my plan. I'm open and ready for Yours."

God never asks us to take the next step alone. When He calls us into something new, He also goes before us.

Change can feel uncomfortable. But God hasn't called us to comfort; He's called us to trust. Let's be women who don't fear the future. Let's be women who walk boldly into it, trusting that when God says He's doing something new, He means it. And it's going to be beautiful.

APPLYING GOD'S TRUTH

1. Is there a change in your life that feels scary or uncertain? Write it down, and beside it, write Isaiah 43:19 as a reminder that God is already at work in it.

2. What is one "next faithful step" you sense God might be inviting you to take, even if you can't see the whole path yet?

3. Take a moment to physically open your hands as you pray today. What are you surrendering to God in this season of change?

A PRAYER FOR TODAY

Father, change is hard. You know how tightly I cling to what's familiar, even when you're gently leading me somewhere new. Help me open my hands. Help me trust that your plans are good, even when they feel uncertain. Remind me that your presence always goes before me, and that I don't have to see the whole path, just the next step. Thank you for being faithful in the middle of the unknown. I believe you are doing a new thing. Help me to walk forward with courage and peace. Amen.

Day 10
The world says to despair during trials.
God says that with Him, there's hope.

Not only that, but we rejoice in our sufferings, knowing that suffering produces endurance, and endurance produces character, and character produces hope, and hope does not put us to shame, because God's love has been poured into our hearts through the Holy Spirit who has been given to us.

- ROMANS 5:3–5

There's a story I like to tell from early on in our marriage. We've lived in Birmingham, Alabama, for almost our entire marriage. It's a wonderful city, full of trails and parks. There is no shortage of places to walk or run.

One day, Andy and I were running together on a local trail. Neither of us has ever been a particularly fast runner, but we've always enjoyed jogging or walking. On this day, we were doing a five-mile run, training for a race we had signed up for.

It was hot and humid (classic Alabama weather), and we were getting close to the end of our run. I was exhausted. Andy was, too, but there's a difference between us: he's a former Marine. That means he has a whole other reserve he can tap into when he gets tired, a mental toughness that was honed during his service.

While I'm tough in certain areas, I wouldn't say exercise is where my toughness shines the brightest. As we hit the last quarter mile, I started slowing down. Everything in me hurt, and I was drenched in sweat and just wanted it to end.

Meanwhile, Andy, in true Marine fashion, started giving me a pep talk. He was saying all these motivational phrases, trying to help me finish our goals for the day. And while I appreciated the heart behind it, in the moment? It was making me more overwhelmed than encouraged.

The line that got me was, "Pain is weakness leaving the body!" That was it. I burst into tears. I told him through sobs, "No more! I am done." The look on his face was priceless. He was so shocked, and then so apologetic. He realized that I was not okay. After we sat for a while (and then even finished the run), I told him how much I appreciated him trying to help, but that I am maybe not a Marine, and his approach did not work for me. (Ha!)

We've laughed about that story so many times over the years. It's a sweet reminder that even when you know and love someone deeply, you can still completely miss what they need in a tough moment. Andy thought he was helping. And he was, kind of. It just wasn't what I needed right then. He was helping me in the way he liked to be helped.

I tell that story because there's a truth about running, lifting weights, or anything that requires growth: you don't get stronger without struggle.

Muscles grow when they're pushed to the point of strain. Distance runners build endurance by running farther than feels comfortable. Strength and growth always come through resistance. No one who's ever run a 5K, 10K, or marathon did it without some discomfort. You grow through the hard stuff.

That same truth, that growth comes through struggle, is also at the heart of our growth as Christians. I've found it to be true over the years: we are never closer to God than when we're walking through a hard season. The easy times make me thankful, but they don't grow me like the tough ones do.

The world doesn't look at hard times this way. There's a whole culture built around the discomfort and pain that trials cause. The world says our struggles are our identity. Our culture often rewards people for staying stuck in their circumstances, for allowing hardship to define who they are. It makes it easy to despair right in the middle of a challenge, and sometimes even to wear that despair like a badge.

The wonderful truth about God and His Word is that there is always hope, the hope that every struggle is a chance to learn more about God and ourselves. We see this throughout Scripture.

One of the places this is on display is in Romans 5. At the beginning of Romans 5, Paul says that because we've been made right with God through faith, we now live at peace with Him. Through Jesus, we've been welcomed into a life of grace, and we stand firm in it, full of joy and hope as we look forward to sharing in God's glory. But Paul isn't done. He builds on this. He writes, "Not only that, but we rejoice in our sufferings, knowing that suffering produces endurance, and endurance produces character, and character produces hope, and hope does not put us to shame, because God's love has been

poured into our hearts through the Holy Spirit who has been given to us"
(vs. 3–5).

Don't miss that: we rejoice in our suffering. What a crazy concept! What
a counter-cultural way to approach suffering. Why would we approach our
tough times with joy? Because of what tough times produce in those who are in
Christ. Paul says that we grow through our trials. Our tough times produce endurance in us, just like the runner who must suffer through countless training
runs to finally prepare for the big race. Endurance produces character. When
we walk with God through trials, our character matures and strengthens. And
when we have come through the other side, it gives us hope that God has seen
us through today's trial and will see us through tomorrow's.

Paul ends this passage by saying that any hope we put in God will be rewarded.
Our hope in God is never in vain. If our strength wavers in tough times, the
Holy Spirit is within us to rekindle that hope.

Tough times aren't fun. If they were, they wouldn't be tough. But we don't
despair like the world does. With a faith rooted in the person and work of
God, and empowered by His Spirit, we face trials with hope, knowing that God
is with us.

APPLYING GOD'S TRUTH

1. How has God used a past season of suffering or difficulty to produce
   endurance and deepen your faith?

2. When you're in the middle of a trial, what helps you shift your mindset from despair to hope?

3. Take a moment to reflect on a recent challenge or difficulty. It could
   be something small or significant. Write down how you initially re-
   sponded, whether with worry, stress, or prayer. Spend time in prayer,
   surrendering this challenge to God and asking for His guidance and
   provision.

A PRAYER FOR TODAY

Father, thank you for every trial; you are working for my good. Help me to trust that suffering is not wasted in your hands but used to grow endurance, character, and hope. When I feel weak or overwhelmed, remind me of your presence and pour your love into my heart through your Spirit. Let my hope in you never waver, because you are always faithful. Amen.

Day 11
The world says no love lasts forever.
God says His love is unfailing.

No, in all these things we are more than conquerors through him who loved us. For I am sure that neither death nor life, nor angels nor rulers, nor things present nor things to come, nor powers, nor height nor depth, nor anything else in all creation, will be able to separate us from the love of God in Christ Jesus our Lord.

- ROMANS 8:37-39

Friend, does this sound familiar?

Love fades.

People change.

Nothing lasts forever.

These words echo through movies, lyrics, and headlines. It's the world's anthem. And the world has moved far away from the hope of unconditional, eternal love.

The message can feel loud and relentless: Don't get your hopes up. Don't give too much. Protect your heart. The heart behind these messages we encounter all the time is a picture of fragile, fleeting, and conditional love.

But God's love? Oh, it is nothing like this version.

Throughout Scripture, God is not just described as loving; He is love. And not the kind that comes and goes. His love is unfailing, which means it's unbreakable. It's not based on your performance. It doesn't shift with seasons. It doesn't diminish on your hard days or disappear when you're struggling. It holds steady, strong, and sure.

Romans 8 gives us one of the most powerful declarations of this truth. Paul doesn't leave room for loopholes or "what ifs." He names every possible barrier: death, life, angels, demons, fears of today or worries about tomorrow, and declares with bold confidence that nothing can separate us from the love of God in Christ Jesus.

Let that sink in: Nothing. Can. Separate. You. And. God.

God's love is not a feeling or a phase. It's the eternal posture of a Father who chose you, adopted you, and delights in you. It's the "everlasting" beneath every breath you take. Jesus Himself says it plainly in John 15:9, "As the Father has loved me, so have I loved you. Abide in my love." He's not asking us to earn His love; He's inviting us to rest in it.

Still, for many of us, it's hard to trust in the kind of love that stays.

The only way I've gotten close to understanding this kind of love is by doing something I love to do whenever I get the chance. Living in Birmingham, Alabama, means we're just a few hours' drive from the coast. We go as often as we can. Whenever we go, I love to get off a little by myself and stand at the ocean's shore, looking out as far as my eyes can see. I look to the left. I look to the right. And the ocean goes on and on, as far as the eye can see. That's what God's love is like! Endless, vast, and beyond comprehension. There's no beginning we can find, and no edge we can reach. It surrounds us. And God invites us into this sustaining, perfect love.

So, what do we do with a love like this? How do we respond?

We stop striving, we stop measuring God's love by our circumstances, and we live like God's adopted daughters. We walk forward anchored in our Father's unwavering, unfailing, unshakable love.

Take a deep breath. Imagine for a moment what your life might look like if you truly believed, deep down to your bones, that you are fully known and fully loved. What burden could you lay down? What fear might finally loosen its grip?

You are more than a conqueror, not through your strength, but through the One who loves you with a love that will never let you go.

APPLYING GOD'S TRUTH

1. Where in your life are you tempted to believe love is conditional or temporary? How does God's promise in Romans 8:37–39 challenge that belief?

2. What would it look like today to rest in, rather than strive for, God's love? What habit or mindset might need to shift?

3. How can you reflect God's unfailing love to someone who may feel unlovable or forgotten right now?

A PRAYER FOR TODAY

Father, thank you for a love that never fades, never fails, and never lets go. When the world whispers that I'm too much or not enough, remind me that your love is unshakable. Help me rest in your love today and receive it fully. Let your love steady my heart and soften how I see others. May I live with boldness and peace, knowing nothing can separate me from your love in Christ Jesus. Amen.

Day 12
The world says to be afraid.
God says to be courageous.

The LORD is my light and my salvation; whom shall I fear? The LORD is the stronghold of my life; of whom shall I be afraid?

- PSALM 27:1

Have you ever had to walk into a social gathering or work conference all by yourself? Isn't it much easier to go to functions like these with a friend or family member? Not long ago, I had the privilege of attending a work conference in Franklin, TN, that I was excited about. When I received the invitation, I immediately knew I wanted to go. But then I realized I wouldn't know anyone there. I started to get nervous; I asked myself, "Who will I talk to at the event? Would I be left out of the conversation at dinner?" Isn't it funny the things we worry about sometimes?

Maybe you haven't faced these exact challenges, but I'm guessing fear has crept in at some point. It's hard not to be in a world filled with uncertainties, big things like wars, financial struggles, and identity crises, but also the everyday worries of getting too much sun, not getting enough sun, juggling responsibilities, etc. While we want to be aware of the world around us, Jesus gently reminds us that we don't have to stay stuck in fear. He calls us to live with courage, trusting that He is with us in it all.

Throughout the Bible, God is clear: He equips us to be bold people. That is our heritage as God's children.

When God called Joshua to replace Moses as the leader of His chosen people, the main point of Joshua's calling was for Joshua to be brave: "Have I not commanded you? Be strong and courageous. Do not be frightened, and do not be dismayed, for the LORD your God is with you wherever you go" (Joshua 1:9). What was the reason Joshua could be strong, courageous, brave and confident? God's presence.

In 2 Timothy 1:7, Paul writes to his young protégé, "For God has not given us a spirit of fear, but of power and of love and of a sound mind." This was Paul trying to encourage Timothy, but it could be just as easily said about Joshua as it could be about us.

In Psalm 27:1, David asks the rhetorical question, "Why should I be afraid"?
He answers it perfectly: "The LORD is my light and my salvation; whom
shall, I fear? The LORD is the stronghold of my life; of whom shall I be
afraid?" He is our deliverer, not only in a spiritual sense, but in a practical,
daily one. God goes before us. He goes with you. He watches your back. He
emboldens us to be people of confidence, not of fear.

Let me invite you in a little deeper. Not only do I get anxious about walking
into parties by myself (all the more reason for me to invite friends), but I
have also become increasingly claustrophobic as I have gotten older. I used
to not be bothered by tight, cramped spaces. Not anymore!

Maybe you can relate to this: A few months ago, I had to have an MRI. The
kind (and understanding) technician told me that if I was in there and got
scared, all I had to do was push the button and she would pull me out.

I didn't think I'd need it. I was feeling brave. But, when I got in that nar-
row, little tube with all that noise, I panicked! Even though I was praying,
my thoughts got the best of me, and I got scared.

So, I pushed the button. The tech came on the speaker and asked me if,
instead of being pulled out and stopping the procedure, I'd like Andy, who
had accompanied me and was waiting in the waiting room, to come stand
at the opening of the MRI tube. So, he came in, and they resumed the test.
I turned my head so I could see about 50% of him, and his presence calmed
me. I made it through it.

I'll be transparent with you, friend: I was confused and a little frustrated
with myself after it was over. I asked myself why my husband's presence
was calming enough that I could continue with the MRI, but my prayers
weren't? I realized that it was because, in that moment, when my anxiety
and fear overwhelmed me, it didn't feel like God was there. I knew in my
head He was there. I know that His Spirit lives within me and His presence
surrounds us. But in that moment when I felt afraid (even though rationally
I knew there was nothing to be afraid of), how I felt didn't match up with
what I knew.

I was reminded of the words from the father in Mark 9:24, who asked Jesus
to heal his son: "I believe; help my unbelief!" God is with us, really with us.
We can believe. We can have faith. In Him, we have the power to be brave;
we simply must believe it.

Today, ask God to remind you how He's been with you. His boldness is a gift he gives to us as His children. The world says there is much to be afraid of. God says we can be bold because He goes with us.

APPLYING GOD'S TRUTH

1. Write down a recent or memorable experience where you felt afraid or anxious, like my examples of attending the work conference or undergoing the MRI. Describe how you felt beforehand and what thoughts went through your mind.

2. Think about moments when you felt God's presence during those times of fear. How did you experience His comfort or guidance? Write down any specific prayers you said or scriptures you remembered that helped calm your fears.

3. Read Psalm 27:1 again ("The LORD is my light and my salvation; whom shall I fear? The LORD is the stronghold of my life; of whom shall I be afraid?"). Write down how this verse relates to your experiences and how it reassures you of God's presence and protection.

A PRAYER FOR TODAY

Father, you are my light and salvation. Help me to trust you more than I trust my fears. When anxiety rises, remind me that you go before me, stand beside me, and watch over me. Strengthen my heart to walk in confidence, knowing that your presence is greater than anything I may face. Amen.

Day 13
The world says hold on tight.
God says to surrender it to Him.

Trust in the LORD with all your heart, and do not lean on your own understanding. In all your ways acknowledge him, and he will make straight your paths.

- PROVERBS 3:5-6

My husband is so handy; it's one of his many gifts. He has a knack for fixing, assembling, or figuring out just about anything. And let me tell you, that's a blessing in my world! Whether it's furniture, organizers, or random decor pieces, I constantly need things put together. The best part is, he's willing to help. I help him with the marketing strategy for his publishing company, and he helps me with all the DIY assembly. It's a sweet balance!

But every now and then, I need something put together and I don't want to bother him; he's got his own work too! If I'm being transparent, though, I hesitate because sometimes I just want to do it myself. There's something satisfying about looking at a project, like a newly built side table or closet organizer, and saying, "I did that! I built that!"

Here's the catch: I'm not exactly "handy." Sure, I've made it work a time or two, but most of the time, if I try to tackle it alone, it doesn't go as planned. And that's perfectly OK. We all have different gifts, right? I'm sure you can relate. The truth is, I get into trouble when I try to hold onto things I'm better off asking for help with.

We all have the tendency to hold on to things we should let go of, and this is true in so many areas of our lives. Some of this tendency is due to our human nature; we may not want to surrender certain things because we feel we're the best person to handle them. And sometimes, that's true. But we often hold on to things because that's what the world tells us to do.

Our culture really values self-sufficiency, doesn't it? We love stories of people who push through, of people overcoming challenges. "Pull yourself up by your bootstraps!" It's almost like we're expected to handle everything on our own. Asking for help? That can still feel like a sign of weakness. The world says it values mental health and self-care, but the sad truth is that it only does so if it doesn't inconvenience anyone else.

The reality is that so many of us carry burdens too heavy to bear alone. From work stress to family struggles, self-doubt, health issues, and everything in between, it all adds up. And yet, the world says, "Hold on tight, do the best you can, and hope it all works out."

But I want to remind you, friend, you don't have to carry it all on your own. Thankfully, oh so thankfully, that's not the way God works.

God is many things. And, so much of who He is centers around His role as burden-lifter. Over and over again in Scripture, God calls us to surrender our cares and concerns to Him. One of the places we see this is in Psalm 55:22. "Cast your burden on the Lord," writes David, "and he will sustain you; he will never permit the righteous to be moved." Cast your burden on the Lord! What a wonderful counter to the logic of the world.

The opposite of holding on tight is letting go. God wants us to step out from the burden of our concerns and surrender the weight to Him. Matthew 11, one of the most comforting promises in the Bible, shows God's heart for those of us who are tired: "Come to me, all who labor and are heavy laden, and I will give you rest" (Matthew 11:28–30). What a promise!

If I'm honest, this one can be tough for me. I tend to cling to things, believing I can solve them on my own or find the right solution under my own power. If I think hard enough and plan long enough, I can devise a solution to my problems. It's not that I doubt God's wisdom or sovereignty; it's just that letting go is challenging for me.

I notice this especially when I struggle to slow down long enough to redirect my thoughts to God and His plans. Most days, I just keep moving ahead. I don't stop long enough to ask, "What am I carrying that I could give to God"? Some days, I rush from when I wake to when my workday ends. I can go for days like this, relying on my knowledge and understanding, just pushing forward, looking at what's in front of me, and not addressing what's sustaining me.

Proverbs 3:5–6 says, "Trust in the LORD with all your heart, and do not lean on your own understanding. In all your ways acknowledge him, and he will make straight your paths." Before we can surrender our burdens, we must trust the one we are surrendering to. Do you trust God to carry your burdens? Do you believe His understanding of our lives, needs, and future is better than our own? We won't give in and give up until we do.

APPLYING GOD'S TRUTH

1. What are you currently holding onto that you know God is asking you to surrender? Why do you think it's hard to let go?

2. How have you seen God carry your burdens in the past? What did you learn about His strength and care for you?

3. Proverbs 3:5–6 encourages us to trust God over our own understanding. What does trusting God practically look like in your daily life right now?

A PRAYER FOR TODAY

Father, thank you for lifting our burdens, straightening our paths, and providing a source of rest when life feels overwhelming. Forgive us for the times we cling too tightly to control, relying on our own understanding instead of trusting in yours. Help us loosen our grip and place our concerns in your hands. In Jesus' name, Amen.

Day 14
The world says being alone means being lonely. God says there is comfort in His presence.

Where shall I go from your Spirit? Or where shall I flee from your presence? If I ascend to heaven, you are there! If I make my bed in Sheol, you are there! If I take the wings of the morning and dwell in the uttermost parts of the sea, even there your hand shall lead me, and your right hand shall hold me.

- PSALM 139:7–10

If it were possible to drive out into the middle of nowhere, as far away from people as it were possible to get, you'd still not be alone. Why? Because God would be there with you. And that, my friend, is a powerful truth.

Being an extrovert myself, which you've probably picked up on if you've spent time with me, whether in real life or virtually, I thrive on being around others. Andy is an introvert. And after more than two decades of marriage, I've learned so much about these labels we toss around.

The biggest lesson? Being an extrovert or introvert isn't about whether you love people, but how you recharge your social batteries. Spending time with a group of people fills my tank. I leave a dinner party or gathering full of energy, sometimes needing extra time to wind down before I can think about sleeping. Being with people fuels me.

Andy is the opposite. He loves people deeply, but social settings drain him. Not because he finds them exhausting or doesn't enjoy them, but simply because that's how he's wired. While I recharge in the presence of others, he finds renewal in quiet moments alone or with a small, close-knit group.

And you know what? That's OK! Maybe you're like him. Maybe solitude fills your cup in a way that a crowded room never could. Both are appreciated. Knowing how you (and your loved ones) are wired is a gift. It helps set expectations, deepens understanding, and makes room for grace. And in a world that often glorifies constant socializing, it's a good reminder: rest and restoration don't look the same for everyone.

I've been thinking about something lately, about this quiet but persistent message in the world around us that being alone means being lonely. Somehow, if you're by yourself, you must be missing out or not measuring up.

And sure, we see posts celebrating solo moments, things like "self-care weekends" or "solo travel," but let's be honest: most of what we see paints togetherness as the goal. Reels filled with friend groups laughing over coffee, couples strolling down charming streets, and families gathered around perfect holiday tables. Even commercials rarely show someone truly alone, because let's face it, brands don't market their products by saying, "Buy this and go be lonely!" No, they tell us, "Buy this and you'll belong."

It's no wonder that so many of us feel that little ache when we find ourselves alone, like we've somehow fallen behind or are missing out. Into this cultural context, God speaks. And what He says is that being alone isn't the same as being lonely. And even more than that, being alone doesn't mean you're unseen.

God's presence isn't dependent on a packed schedule or a full room. He meets us in the quiet, in the in-between, in the moments when no one else is around. Psalm 16:11 reminds us, "In Your presence, there is fullness of joy." It is not just a little joy; it is a fullness of joy that doesn't require an invitation to the party or the perfect group of friends.

God's Word contains two powerful truths that change our entire perspective on loneliness. First, there is the fundamental truth that if we're in Christ, we're never alone. If we have been saved by faith in the person and work of Jesus, there is never a place where we can go that God isn't. David sums this up perfectly in Psalm 139:7–10: "Where shall I go from your Spirit? Or where shall I flee from your presence? If I ascend to heaven, you are there! If I make my bed in Sheol, you are there! If I take the wings of the morning and dwell in the uttermost parts of the sea, even there your hand shall lead me, and your right hand shall hold me."

But the most powerful truth is that with God, you don't have to ever feel lonely, because He is enough. Isaiah 41:10 encourages us to "fear not," and to "be not dismayed." Why? Because God is with us! "I will strengthen you," God says. "I will help you; I will uphold you with my righteous right hand." Deuteronomy 31:6 tells us to "Be strong and courageous. Do not fear or be in dread of them, for it is the Lord your God who goes with you. He will not leave you or forsake you." In Matthew 28:20, Jesus says to the disciples, "... And behold, I am with you always, to the end of the age." God's presence sustains and upholds us. We are never lonely because we are never alone.

Will you feel lonely sometimes? Probably. We're human, and feelings can mislead us. That little voice may whisper that God is distant or that we're alone, but that's not true. God's presence isn't a feeling; it's a promise. He is unchanging, constant, and near, always.

So, when loneliness creeps in, rest in this truth and let His peace fill the space where doubt tries to settle. If today finds you in a quiet place, take heart. You are not alone; you are held.

APPLYING GOD'S TRUTH

1. When do you most often feel lonely, and how can you remind yourself of God's constant presence in those moments?

2. How does the truth of Psalm 139:7–10 challenge the way you view solitude?

3. What practical steps can you take this week to find comfort in God's presence, especially in quiet or isolated moments?

A PRAYER FOR TODAY

Lord, thank you that I am never truly alone. Even when I feel unseen or isolated, remind me that your presence surrounds and sustains me. Help me rest in the truth that you are enough and that there is fullness of joy in your presence. Amen.

Day 15
The world says people should pay for their missteps. God says to meet others with grace and mercy.

The steadfast love of the Lord never ceases; His mercies never come to an end; they are new every morning; great is your faithfulness.

- LAMENTATIONS 3:22-23

Getting caught up in the world's view of failure is so easy. If you make a mistake, you're wearing a permanent label. If you fall short, the world will never let you forget it. This mentality is all around us, whether in how we judge ourselves or others. It's this unforgiving view where mistakes are met with punishment, and there is no room for second chances. But thank goodness, that's not how God sees us.

God's Word repeatedly reminds us that while our missteps have consequences, He never sees us through the lens of failure. The world might hold us to a standard of perfection, but God meets us with grace and mercy, over and over again. When we make mistakes, God doesn't abandon us or label us unworthy. He offers us the same mercy that He shows others. His love for us is steadfast, and His mercies are new every morning, no matter what.

In this broken world, we're constantly faced with moments when people let us down or when we mess up. It's easy to fall into the trap of thinking we, or others, don't deserve grace. But grace isn't something we earn. It's a gift. When we start meeting others with the same grace that God extends to us, we begin to see people, even in their brokenness, as loved and redeemable. And that includes ourselves.

I will never forget a ministry season when Andy and I were a small part of seeing grace extended to people who deeply needed it. There is an incredible ministry in Birmingham called Lifeline Children's Services. They do so much amazing work that I don't have space to describe it. But one of the programs they have is a biblically-based, discipleship-driven parenting class for parents who have had their children removed by child services. For parents who want to work to regain custody of their children, part of the work they must do is to take court-ordered parenting classes. Lifeline has lobbied the state to allow them to provide courses that teach these parents a biblically-based parenting model. The incredible thing is that it's driven by the local church, where members can surround these parents with love and care as they strive to get their lives back on track.

Andy and I spent 8 weeks teaching a group of 6 mothers who had all had their children taken from them. The decisions and lifestyle many of these women were leading had consequences for them and their children. And to a person, each of them owned their mistakes and worked incredibly hard to overcome them. These women were in the hardest moment of their lives, trying to rebuild, prove they were trustworthy again, and right the wrongs they had committed. Every week, we listened to their stories. And every week, we heard echoes of the same heartbreaking belief:

"I don't deserve to be their mom."

"I'm just a failure."

"I'm not worth fighting for."

But those weren't the final words. Most of the women did the work. Most regained custody of their children and set their lives back on the right path. In at least two cases, these women embraced the support and love our church members offered them in the midst of their struggles. One woman was baptized in our church and now attends with her children. Her actions had consequences, but the grace and love that were extended to her changed her and her children's lives.

You see, the words these women were saying about themselves were born out of a fallen world where we're told we can't overcome our mistakes. But the thing about those words is that they weren't true, not in light of the Gospel.

Scripture tells a different story to us, a story of grace that reaches low and mercy that never runs out. When we place our faith in Jesus, we aren't defined by what we've done or what's been done to us. We are defined by who He is and what He has done on our behalf. God doesn't see us through a lens of failure, but through the lens of the cross. He sees us through Jesus. Titus 3:5 says, "He saved us, not because of works done by us in righteousness, but according to his own mercy." Mercy was the motivating factor for God's rescue of us. And the beautiful thing is that God meets us with grace, not just once. Over and over again.

Lamentations 3:22–23 says, "The steadfast love of the Lord never ceases; his mercies never come to an end; they are new every morning; great is your faithfulness." Let these familiar verses sink in. God's love never ceases. Ever. It doesn't stop when we hurt people or are hurt by people. There is no end to His mercy. It doesn't end when we let someone down, and it doesn't end when someone lets us down. His faithfulness never lessens. It doesn't lessen when, we wrong someone, and it doesn't lessen when someone wrongs us.

I do not know what happened to each mom in that class. But they experienced grace and love in the face of the crippling consequences of their missteps. For at least a few of them, it seemed to make all the difference in their redemption and reconciliation.

You may be walking through life carrying a label someone else gave you. Or one you gave yourself. But God gives you a new name. You may see someone in your life who's fallen short, whom you think doesn't deserve a second chance. But grace wasn't meant to be deserved. It was meant to be given. So the next time you're tempted to write someone off, or write yourself off, listen closer. The world says, "Make them pay." God says, "I've already paid on their behalf."

His mercy is new every morning. Even for you. Even for them.

APPLYING GOD'S TRUTH

1. What is a label you've been carrying, maybe one the world gave you or one you've given yourself, that God wants to replace with His truth?

2. Who needs to be reminded that grace is real and mercy is for them, not just for everyone else? How can you tell them this truth?

3. What's one practical way you can extend grace this week to someone who doesn't "deserve" it?

A PRAYER FOR TODAY

Father, thank you for your mercies that never run out. Thank you for seeing me not as a list of my mistakes, but as your beloved child, wrapped in grace. Help me to see others the same way. When I'm tempted to hold someone's past against them, or my own, remind me of the cross. Remind me that no one is ever too far gone for redemption. Amen.

Day 16
The world says to worry about your needs.
God says that He will meet all of them.

He who did not spare his own Son but gave him up for us all, how will he not also with him graciously give us all things?

- ROMANS 8:32

When our children were young, Andy and I felt God leading him and one of his close friends to start a youth ministry organization from scratch. They worked hard and raised investor capital to launch the ministry, but once it was launched, they would earn a living through the curriculum and Bible study resources they sold to churches. Their resources were terrific, but the problem was that no one knew who they were!

They worked hard in those early years, and the ministry grew. But times were lean. We had shrunk our family budget to fit his income, but there was still barely enough, most months, to make ends meet. God was good; we were getting by, but just barely.

I remember one month, almost two years in, when the ministry had grown significantly. We were not out of the financial woods yet, and would not be for several more years, but things were looking up. It was then that a significant expense came up. I cannot even recall what it was, but it was a lot of money.

I remember standing in our garage on a Saturday afternoon, crying because we were literally out of money. I think we had twenty or thirty dollars left in our checking account. They had worked so hard to be faithful; as a family, we had made sacrifices to make it work. And it was looking like it was not going to work.

We discussed our options. I remember Andy talking about taking a second job. We talked about borrowing money from family, but we just did not feel comfortable with it. We were worried about how and where to find the money to cover our needs, plus this emergency expense. So, we continued to pray about it and wait for the Lord to show us what was next.

The next afternoon, Andy's aunt unexpectedly dropped by our house. We visited for a while, and then she said, "Well, I dropped by because your great-aunt is getting her affairs in order before she passes, and she wanted to give you something."

Andy had a great-aunt he did not know that well; he may have only seen her once every few years. She was nearing the end of her life and decided to distribute some of her estate while she was still living. We expressed our gratitude, and Andy's aunt handed us the check.

When she left, we opened it together. We could not believe it; the amount was exactly what we needed to cover the emergency (plus a little more to help us over the next few months).

Over our two-plus decades of marriage, we have had similar instances. Sometimes, it has been money. Sometimes, a door has opened or closed. Sometimes, it has been a conversation or an unexpected interaction. But time after time, we have seen God consistently provide for our needs, often in the most unexpected ways.

God has met our needs, and over time, our surprise at His provision has lessened. Why? Because God has already shown us over and over that He is faithful. We are not surprised when God acts in accordance with His character. However, we are always deeply thankful and full of gratitude and awe.

We worry about meeting our needs—today's and tomorrow's—because we are human and because the world around us conditions us to worry.

Think about how many products are designed to meet needs. Think about the endless commercials about retirement and savings plans. The promise of financial security is everywhere because our culture knows we are desperate to feel that we have enough. How many conversations do you have that center on worry of some sort? We worry about our health, our children's college expenses, our 401K, and so on. We are prone to worry. And at the heart of our worry is an unstated question about God's ability to do what He says He will do.

God is the need-meeter. There are so many places in the Bible where we see this. In the Sermon on the Mount, Jesus says, "Therefore do not be anxious, saying, 'What shall we eat?' or 'What shall we drink?'

. . . But seek first the kingdom of God and his righteousness, and all these things will be added to you" (Matthew 6:31–33). The Apostle Paul stands on this very promise when he wrote in Philippians 4:19, "And my God will supply every need of yours according to his riches in glory in Christ Jesus." Paul could say that to the Philippians because he knew it to be true in his own life.

My favorite place in the Bible where we see God promise to meet our needs is from the Apostle Paul. Inspired by the Holy Spirit, Paul wrote in his letter to the Romans, "He who did not spare his own Son but gave him up for us all, how will he not also with him graciously give us all things?" (Romans 8:32). What Paul is saying here is fantastic. He is saying that because God has already given us the most incredible gift He can ever give us and that He did so while we were in rebellion in our sin, why would we think He would be any less likely to continue to meet our needs, especially since if we've come to faith in Christ, we are His children! He gave us Jesus while we were His enemies. How much more will He give us now that we've been adopted into His family!

Friend, if you worry about your needs, take God at His word. Believe that all His promises are "yes and amen"! He will never not meet your needs. Sometimes, He will let you get to the end of your rope so that when He finally does step in, there can be no mistaking who the source of your rescue is. But even when He does this, and let me assure you that He has done it in our lives repeatedly, He does it so that we will draw even closer to our deliverer, trusting and loving Him more because of His powerful and tender provision.

Trust Him. His promises are true. Lean into His love. Let Him be the one who meets every single need you bring to Him.

Because He always will.

APPLYING GOD'S TRUTH

1. What current needs are you most worried about, and how might you surrender those to God in faith today?

2. Can you recall a specific time when God provided for you unexpectedly? How did that experience shape your trust in Him?

3. Share your story of how God has provided in your life with a friend, family member, or small group. Discuss how your experience has deepened your faith and encouraged you to rely more fully on God's promises. Encourage others by reminding them of God's faithfulness in both big and small ways.

A PRAYER FOR TODAY

Father, you are my provider: faithful, generous, and always near. Forgive me when I forget that and give in to worry or fear. Help me to trust your promises and remember that you gave your Son for me, and that nothing I need is too big or too small for you. Teach me to rest in your care today, believing you will meet every need in your perfect timing. Amen.

Day 17
The world says chart your own path.
God says to let Him guide your decisions.

And your ears shall hear a word behind you, saying, "This is the way, walk in it," when you turn to the right or when you turn to the left.

- ISAIAH 30:21

If you've been around here for a while, you might know that my career path hasn't been a straight line; it's looked more like a winding trail with plenty of detours. I started at Auburn University (War Eagle!) as an education major. I'd always imagined myself as an elementary school teacher. I loved children and felt confident that this was where God had placed me.

But during my freshman year, I started to sense a shift. I still loved the heart behind teaching, but the classes weren't lighting a fire in me. That summer, I worked with the North American Mission Board at a trail ride ministry in Wyoming. It was life-giving. I rediscovered how much I loved being outdoors (especially in the mountains of Wyoming) and working with horses.

So back at Auburn that fall, I changed my major to Animal and Dairy Science, with plans to become a large animal vet. I was excited until Organic Chemistry class hit. I'd always been a straight-A student, but that class knocked me off my feet. I began wondering if I'd misunderstood God's direction. Maybe horses were a passion, not a profession.

After more prayer and conversations with my parents and Andy (my boyfriend at the time), I made another shift, this time to Human Development and Family Studies, to become a Marriage and Family Therapist like my dad. I earned my master's degree and practiced for 15 wonderful years.

Then, over seven years ago, everything changed again. What started as a love for decorating my home became a lifestyle brand and full-time career. I didn't plan or study for it, but I can now clearly see how God prepared me for it. Looking back, I can trace His hand in every turn; even the ones that felt like dead ends at the time.

Had I clung to my plan, I may have missed out on meeting my husband, discovering my love for the American West, working as a therapist, or encouraging others through a website and social media platform I cherish so deeply. His path has been far better than mine ever could have been.

One of my favorite verses, Isaiah 30:21, comes in a chapter where God calls His people to trust Him again. Though they'd turned to other sources for help, He responds with grace and the promise of restoration. His voice gently guides: "This is the way, walk in it."

The world tells us to look within for direction, follow our hearts, "you do you," and make our own way. But we don't always know what's best for us. We can't always see what's ahead, and our hearts can be confused or overwhelmed. That's why we need a guide who sees the whole path.

God's way is always better. His guidance is steady, loving, and sure. Psalm 32:8 says, "I will instruct you and teach you in the way you should go; I will counsel you with my eye upon you." That's not a distant God; that's a close and caring one.

Imagine climbing a mountain alone. At first, it feels doable. But then a storm rolls in, and you get lost. Now imagine doing that same climb with a trusted guide who knows the terrain and can walk you through the hardest parts. That's what it looks like to live with God as your guide. We still face challenges, but we're never alone.

I've tried both ways: charging ahead and pausing to listen for His voice. I can tell you that listening is always better. He's never failed me, and He won't fail you either.

The wonderful hymn, "Come Thou Fount of Every Blessing," by Robert Robinson, has a lyric you may have heard and might not know precisely what it means. The line goes, "Here I raise mine Ebenezer; Hither by Thy help I'm come." Do you remember where the reference "Ebeneezer" is from? It's a reference to 1 Samuel 7:12: "Then Samuel took a stone and set it up between Mizpah and Shen and called its name Ebenezer; for he said, 'Till now the Lord has helped us.'" Ebenezer means "stone of help." Samuel set this stone as a physical reminder of God's faithfulness and deliverance after Israel's victory over the Philistines. When we sing "Here I raise my Ebenezer," we say, "Right here, I'm setting a marker to remember how God has helped me." It's a poetic and biblical way of expressing gratitude and dependence on God's ongoing help and faithfulness.

We have some dear friends who have built their own "Ebeneezer" in their backyard. It's just a stack of stones, a rock for every moment they've experienced God's faithfulness. It's a beautiful, tangible reminder of where they've been and how God walked with them. When you have reached a milestone or overcome a tough moment, consider and reflect on how God has been faithful. You might not stack stones in your backyard, but you can recall memories in your heart and let them remind you to keep trusting Him.

God is always guiding your path according to His perfect plan. And the outcome is always for His glory and your good.

APPLYING GOD'S TRUTH

1. Looking back, can you identify a time when God redirected your plans in a way that was better than you had envisioned?

2. What "Ebenezer stones" could you raise in your life, moments when you saw God's hand guiding you?

3. What is a current decision or uncertain step you're facing where you need to pause and listen for God's voice?

A PRAYER FOR TODAY

Lord, thank you for guiding me through every twist and turn. Help me to trust your voice above all others, especially when the way forward is unclear. Remind me of your past faithfulness and give me courage to follow your lead today. May my steps bring glory to you and peace to my heart. Amen.

Day 18
The world says the everyday moments don't matter.
But God says that every moment has meaning.

This is the day that the Lord has made; let us rejoice and be glad in it.

- PSALM 118:24

Her alarm goes off before the sun peeks through the blinds, and before her feet hit the floor, the to-do list is already swirling in her mind. She exhales, wishing for just a few more minutes, but her heart is already racing with all that needs to get done. So, she pushes back the covers, plants her feet on the ground, and steps into the day ahead. She pours her coffee, opens her laptop, and in the quiet of the pre-dawn, knocks out the first tasks of the day before everyone else is awake.

Do you recognize yourself in this description? Honesty time: I know I do. (That's me waving my hand over here!). If this describes you, as it does me sometimes, it should come as no surprise. In life, we're told to go, go, go. The world has taught us to be caught up in this constant race to the next thing. Maybe that's not your specific struggle. But based on the number of conversations I have had with friends and peers, I know many of us have to fight the urge to be and stay busy.

But what if the real win isn't in doing more, but in simply being present? What if the way forward isn't moving faster but soaking up the little moments and finding peace instead of running on empty? The world may rush past the "ordinary," but that's exactly where God meets us: in the everyday moments of each day. And what we often find is that those moments are the ones with the most meaning.

Now, I should say that I am a woman who loves a good to-do list. Checking things off gives me a sense of accomplishment. Running a business keeps me busy, and I take pride in my work. But the moments that feel the most meaningful aren't the big wins; they're the small pauses.

For example, we expect our children to keep their rooms tidy. That's a house rule. But sometimes, if they've slipped a little in this area, I'll take a break from my workday and straighten up their rooms. I turn on praise music, pray over them as I fold a blanket or pick up their clothes, and in that quiet moment, I'm reminded: God is in the ordinary, too. Even the most minor tasks can be a time to reflect on the love and grace of God.

In his letter to the Ephesians, a church he loved dearly, Paul encouraged them to be intentional with their time. He wrote, "Look carefully then how you walk, not as unwise but as wise, making the best use of the time, because the days are evil. Therefore, do not be foolish, but understand what the will of the Lord is" (Ephesians 5:15—17).

Paul understood how easily the days can slip away, either lost in distraction or spent chasing meaning in busyness. But there's a better way. We learn to walk in balance when we seek God's wisdom, embracing purposeful work and meaningful rest. Each day is a gift from God, full of opportunities to love well, live fully, and lean into His purpose for us.

The other day, my best friend, Katy, and I were chatting about our packed schedules when she asked, "Did you leave any white space on your calendar?" She meant those open moments for a last-minute lunch with my husband, Andy, or helping my daughter Caroline after school. It was a reminder I needed, and I am so thankful for a friend who speaks into my life.

Does this mean we should ignore our to-do lists or sit around all day? Of course not. It's a "both/and"; we can work hard and embrace rest. We can move forward and slow down when needed. Because God sees the meaning in every moment, especially the ones the world calls mundane.

A full to-do list isn't the only sign of a productive day. Sometimes, the most meaningful moments happen in the margins. Whether it's sipping coffee with your spouse, listening to a friend on a walk, or simply sitting outside and taking it all in, make room for the small moments of grace. After all, maybe the most important moments aren't the ones we plan but the ones we make room for.

APPLYING GOD'S TRUTH

1. How can you intentionally create space in your daily schedule to embrace the "white space" moments and allow for meaningful interruptions?

2. What "mundane" tasks could be transformed into acts of worship or opportunities to glorify God? How might this change your perspective on those tasks?

3. Reflect on your current priorities: Are you more focused on checking off tasks or making room for moments of rest and connection with others? How might you adjust this balance?

A PRAYER FOR TODAY

Father, help me slow down and see you in the ordinary moments of my day. Teach me to use my time wisely, not just for productivity but for presence, rest, and opportunities to love others well. Let me find joy in the small, sacred moments, knowing that every moment with you has meaning. Amen.

Day 19
The world says you define your own identity.
God says that your identity is in Him.

I have been crucified with Christ. It is no longer I who live, but Christ who lives in me. And the life I now live in the flesh I live by faith in the Son of God, who loved me and gave himself for me.

- GALATIANS 2:20

We are so blessed to have three daughters. Our son is also a blessing, but as I am writing this for women, I can't help but think of our girls. As you can imagine, over the years we have had (and still do have) many conversations revolving around appearances. When our girls were younger, we heard that everything would be better if they only had curly hair and not straight hair. I remember one of them saying that if she could JUST go to Homecoming with this one guy, then people would see her as popular. Another time, I recall a conversation where someone didn't like being tall (it's hard to remember who said it because they're all tall). They wished they were more petite like their friends. Maybe this sounds familiar to you.

This struggle often extends to my own thoughts, linking happiness to shedding the last 10 pounds or achieving specific business goals. These moments have me questioning how deeply we internalize these beliefs, even as grown women.

Do we believe our identity is based on performance? Do we believe external appearances or career success define who we are? The beautiful news is that no matter what the world around us tries to tell us, and no matter what we try to tell ourselves, God's Word has spoken. The Bible unequivocally tells us that our identities have nothing to do with our appearance or our performance.

Read Galatians 2:20. Paul wrote the Galatians to help them understand their freedom as new creations in Christ. These new believers had come to faith in Jesus and were trying to live out their faith as well as they knew how. However, they had been getting off course in their faith, and Paul wanted to remind them of some essential truths.

Look what Paul says to the Galatians here. He helps them see how his former, world-based identity was put to death when he came to saving faith in Jesus. Paul knew that the way he once understood his status and worth had forever changed. His identity would forever be found solely in who he was in Christ. And Paul understood that this new identity was a gift given to him. As he wrote in 2 Corinthians 5:17, he was a "new creation."

How comforting this truth is to us! Our hearts can sing because we are free from being defined by the external measures our world uses to pin people's identities on them. So, while our world says our identities are found in our appearance, God says our identities are rooted in Him. While the world says our identities are defined by our children (or lack thereof), God says we identify as His children! The world might say that success, money, status, or stuff is how we think about our identity. God says who we are as born-again Christ-followers is how we understand who we are and where our value is.

When you are bombarded by the endless messages of the world about who you are or who you are not, quiet the noise and rest in Jesus. Stop looking to your achievements, social media presence, or family roles to measure how you add up. Instead, think of the unparalleled sense of peace that comes when we know that our identity is hidden in Christ.

APPLYING GOD'S TRUTH

1. Identify common lies you believe about your identity (e.g., "I am only valuable if I am successful" or "I need to look a certain way to be loved"). For each lie, find and write a corresponding biblical truth that counters it. Keep this list handy and review it daily, especially during moments of self-doubt.

2. What voices or influences in your life tend to shape your beliefs the most? How can you be more intentional about filtering everything through the unchanging truth of God's Word?

3. What daily habits or disciplines can you put in place to ensure that your heart and mind are consistently filled with the truth of Scripture rather than the shifting messages of the world?

A PRAYER FOR TODAY

Father, in a world filled with uncertainty and confusion, help me to stand firm on your unchanging truth. Guard my heart and mind from the lies of the world and draw me deeper into your Word so that I may know and trust you more. May the Spirit guide me to walk in wisdom, confidence, and faith, always anchored in the truth of who You are. Amen.

Day 20
The world says you are beyond forgiveness.
God says that you are never too far gone to be forgiven.

He does not deal with us according to our sins, nor repay us according to our iniquities. For as high as the heavens are above the earth, so great is his steadfast love toward those who fear him; as far as the east is from the west, so far does he remove our transgressions from us.

- PSALM 103:10-12

Les Misérables was the first Broadway play I saw growing up, and I was completely mesmerized. The way so many stories unfold within the bigger story felt so magical and expansive to me. It was just incredible. Our family played the soundtrack around our house when I was young, and someone was always singing along. The play and the novel by Victor Hugo hold such a special place in my heart.

If you've seen the play or read the book, you'll remember one of the early scenes where Jean Valjean, a recently released ex-convict, is taken in by a kind bishop who offers him a meal and shelter. But in the night, Valjean steals the bishop's silver and flees.

Caught and brought back by the police, Valjean is certain of his fate. He knows he's going back to prison. But instead of accusing him, the bishop does something radical. He tells the officers the silver was a gift. Then, remarkably, he hands Valjean his most valuable candlesticks, insisting he take them, too. This powerful moment of grace changes Valjean's heart and sets his life on a remarkable course.

It's hard to put into words what a powerful scene this is; even writing this almost brings tears to my eyes. The bishop had every right to demand justice. Instead, he chose mercy, offering his best to the one who had betrayed him.

Can you relate to what Valjean must have been feeling in that merciful moment? Do you ever feel like your sin weighs you down? Do you ever feel burdened by the shame and guilt you know you deserve? If so, you're not the first to ever feel this way.

Our world impresses upon us that mercy is a luxury. Even if we're shown mercy once, it has its limits. Plus, we know ourselves better than anyone. We know our thoughts, our actions, our hearts. We know our past. And if we're not careful, we can believe the lies of the world that say our pasts and sins define us.

How wonderful is the truth of God's Word, which says that in Christ, our sin will never define us.

Take a moment and read Psalm 103:10–12. This is one of four psalms in a row written by David that praise God for how He has interacted with His people in the past. The heart of the psalm is verses 6–14, where David speaks of the mercy with which God deals with us, His people. Our sin deserves judgment. That's the only response from a holy, just God. But through faith in Jesus, what we receive from God is mercy. We receive forgiveness. Are you following the beauty of this love our God has for us?

In Les Misérables, Valjean couldn't process the bishop's kindness. He couldn't understand it. He knew he didn't deserve it. And yet, it ended up being part of what transformed Valjean's life. Maybe you live with similar feelings. Maybe you have been holding on to your past sins and failures. Maybe you have been living a life that feels burdened with shame and guilt. Maybe, like Jean Valjean, you struggle to accept mercy. If this describes you, know that the grace and forgiveness God offers you in Jesus is 100% complete and total. As David says, God "removes" your transgressions as far as the east is from the west! He doesn't save them for later. They're gone forever.

Does God want us to be holy? Absolutely. The standard for being in relationship with God is the same today as it was when He first called the Israelites to Him. God expects perfection. It's the only way He can be in a relationship with us. He is perfectly holy. We must be holy too. How incredibly, wonderfully, powerfully perfect the Gospel is, that God in His mercy and love counts Jesus' righteousness on behalf of those who profess faith in Him. And when we do, we are forgiven for our sins, not just once, but forevermore. This is amazing love!

Listen to these words. Tune your ears to His forgiveness of you. In Christ, you are never beyond forgiveness. Come to Him today.

APPLYING GOD'S TRUTH

1. Are there past mistakes or sins you struggle to believe God has fully forgiven? How does Psalm 103:10–12 challenge how you see God's mercy toward you?

2. How does truly accepting God's forgiveness free you to live differently? What would it look like to walk in the confidence of knowing your sins are completely removed in Christ?

3. Is there someone in your life who needs the same kind of mercy and forgiveness that God has shown you? How can you reflect His grace by extending forgiveness to others today?

A PRAYER FOR TODAY

Father, thank you for your boundless mercy and grace that removes my sins as far as the east is from the west. Help me to fully embrace the forgiveness you have given me in Christ and to walk in freedom instead of shame. Teach me to extend that same grace to others, reflecting your love in my life.
Amen.

Day 21
The world says more is better.
God says to be content with what you have.

*Keep your life free from love of money, and be content with what you have,
for he has said, "I will never leave you nor forsake you."*

- HEBREWS 13:5

I don't know about you, but it feels like the world around us is working pretty hard to make us feel like we're missing out on something. We're constantly exposed to someone trying to sell us the next best thing. Social media nudges us to compare ourselves to others, leaving us feeling like we fall short. It all adds up. It can make the idea of being content feel almost impossible. In a world that's always pushing us to want more, do more, and be more, contentment feels like some kind of rebellion, doesn't it?

But here's the beauty of it: so many people are truly content. Have you met someone who radiates peace because of contentment? They've figured out that joy doesn't come from more stuff, but from appreciating what's already right in front of them. I'm not perfect at being content, but when I have those moments where I truly see and appreciate what I have, it's like stepping into a moment of calm. It's like floating from the rush of a fast-moving stream to a peaceful spot where everything feels right.

Contentment is one of those profound topics that makes us pause and reflect. What does it mean to be content? It's that deep sense of peace and happiness with where you are in life. Whether it's with how you look, the things you own, your career, or even your health, contentment is simply saying, "I'm thankful." What contentment doesn't mean is that we stop striving for growth. It merely means that we're grateful for the little things. And honestly, that's a beautiful way to live.

Hebrews 13:5 says, "Keep your life free from love of money, and be content with what you have, for he has said, 'I will never leave you nor forsake you.'" If you only read the first part of that verse, you'd be in good shape. That could be a message written on a billboard or a fortune cookie, and you'd say, "That's good advice." Materialism is wrong, and greed has been the downfall of so many. The message to keep from being overly fixated on money and material things would likely find acceptance among secular audiences. It's the second part of the verse that is the game changer.

True contentment comes from God's presence in our lives. Contentment comes from God's faithfulness. We can resist the love of money and its fleeting promise of comfort and security because God alone satisfies any need we have. He is our portion! He is enough in every sense of the word. If all you had left in your life was the knowledge that you were God's and that you are secure in Him, for now and eternity, that would be enough. It would be more than enough. And that knowledge is where real contentment is found.

Want to know something? Contentment isn't unique to Christians. But perfect contentment is. There are plenty of places where we find satisfaction, peace, and rest in the world, if only for a moment. But only in God are those things perfectly guaranteed. The more we know God, the more we discover this truth.

Our family loves Christmas mornings. I know you're probably thinking, "Brendt, doesn't everyone?" But truly, Christmas mornings in our house are something extra special. We don't just do "mornings;" we stretch them into an all-day celebration, savoring every moment and holding onto them for as long as we can.

Our Christmas mornings have been filled with joy for as long as I can remember. But there were a few years when a little bit of drama crept in. I remember when our middle daughter, Abby, was little, there were a couple of Christmases where she ended up feeling sad after unwrapping her presents. I'll explain. Abby often asked for specific gifts, only to feel disappointed when she didn't get exactly what she had hoped for. But it wasn't just about her gifts; she wanted what her sisters got, too. Being the middle child can be tricky sometimes, right? So, we'd help her process those feelings, and within no time, she'd bounce back. But for a couple of Christmases, it was something we had to navigate.

As Abby grew, her perspective shifted, and I'm so proud of how much she has grown. As she got a little older, she started managing her expectations better and even began asking her sisters what was on their lists, helping her think about her own more thoughtfully. But the real change happened as she matured—she started to embrace gratitude more and compare less. She began to truly appreciate the gifts she received, seeing each one as special and meaningful just for her. And, now, as a young adult, her excitement for seeing everyone else open their presents is contagious.

What Abby experienced growing up is something I think many of us can relate to. We live in a world where we're constantly told we need more; more makeup, bags, clothes, bigger houses, fancier vacations, etc., and we think these things will bring us lasting happiness and joy. But deep down, we know those eventually will fade away. Ecclesiastes 5:10 reminds us, "He who loves money will not be satisfied with money, nor he who loves wealth with his income; this also is vanity." Only God can fill that space in our hearts, and the best part? He fills it perfectly.

APPLYING GOD'S TRUTH

1. Meditate on passages emphasizing contentment and gratitude, such as Philippians 4:11–13 and 1 Thessalonians 5:18. Consider how these verses challenge your perspective on material possessions and fulfillment.

2. Create a gratitude jar by keeping paper and pens close to a jar (like a mason jar or vase). Encourage your family members to drop notes in the jar throughout the day, each note expressing something they are grateful for. At the end of the week, gather together to read aloud these notes and discuss how reflecting on your gratitude has brought more peace and joy into your lives.

A PRAYER FOR TODAY

Father, thank you for being the only source of true and lasting contentment. In a world that constantly tells us we need more to be enough, remind us that you are already more than enough. Teach us to be grateful for what we have and to rest in your faithful presence. May we live each day with open hands and peaceful hearts, anchored in the truth that you will never leave or forsake us. In Jesus' name, Amen.

Day 22
The world says be anxious about the future.
God says to face tomorrow with peace.

Peace, I leave with you; my peace I give to you. Not as the world gives do I give to you. Let not your hearts be troubled, neither let them be afraid.

- JOHN 14:27

There's a unique kind of anxiety that slips in when your children begin stepping into adulthood. As I write this, we're walking with our two daughters through their college years. One is a junior and the other is a sophomore. Their lives revolve around tomorrow. From career choices and internships to friendships, dating, and class schedules, it can feel like a never-ending stream of high-stakes decisions. We're cheering them on every step, but if you're a parent, you know that we carry the weight of it, too. Maybe you're in that season as well?

As a mom, I want to help. And if I'm honest, there are days I want to jump in and fix every dysfunction with my own two hands. I don't know that we ever fully outgrow that urge. But deep down, I know that stepping in is rarely what's best. So much of their lives now are outside my reach, and while that's hard, it's also good. It's an invitation to trust. Still, that space between what we can and can't do? That's where anxiety sneaks in.

Isn't that so often how it is between us and the Lord, too?

Truthfully, anxiety about the future doesn't always come from a single, major crisis. Sometimes it creeps in through the everyday weight of life: the full calendar, the unexpected bill, the argument that didn't get resolved, or the "what if" that plays on a loop in your head. It's the slow build that tightens our shoulders before the day even begins.

But into that mix of anxious thoughts, Jesus speaks a better word: "Peace I leave with you. My peace I give to you." And then, He adds something that changes everything: "Not as the world gives."

That part matters. The world offers peace with conditions; peace if your account is stable, your kids are thriving, your relationships are smooth, and your plans are on track. But that kind of peace is paper-thin. It can go away overnight, and most of us know what that feels like.

Friend, Jesus offers something altogether different. His peace isn't rooted in circumstances. It's rooted in Himself.

Psalm 46:1 says, "God is our refuge and strength, a very present help in trouble." He doesn't just show up once the storm passes. He is very present, right now, in the thick of it. In the traffic jam. At the doctor's office. In the not-yet and the still-waiting. When the "what ifs" are loud, His presence is louder still.

Peace about the future won't come from finally figuring everything out. It comes from trusting God, who already has. Romans 8:28 reminds us, "And we know that for those who love God all things work together for good…" Not all things are good, but God is good in all things. That includes tomorrow, and the day after that, and every unknown in between.

So, let's get practical. What's one thing making you anxious right now? Name it. Bring it to the surface. And then do something that's been life-changing for me: Replace that anxious thought with gratitude. It might feel small, even silly, but I promise, it's powerful. Gratitude doesn't erase the tough times; it just gives you a God-sized perspective.

Instead of "What if my child chooses the wrong path," try "Thank You, Lord, for how You're already at work in her life."

Instead of thinking, "What if I can't hold this together?" pray, "Thank You for being my strength when I feel weak."

You may still feel the anxiety, but now you're training your heart to look through the lens of trust, not fear.

Don't keep this peace to yourself. When you speak peace over someone else's storm, it often takes root in your heart. You don't have to be perfect or have all the answers. Just share what God is showing you, right where you are.

Let Jesus speak peace over the things in your life that stir fear. Let His presence calm your heart more than your circumstances. Let His Word steady you when everything around you feels shaky. Even if the earth gives way, God is our refuge. He is enough. And He is near.

APPLYING GOD'S TRUTH

1. What's one area of your life where anxiety tends to show up most often?

2. What's a specific way you can replace that anxiety with gratitude today?

3. Who's someone you could encourage with God's peace this week?

A PRAYER FOR TODAY

Father, you know how easily my heart drifts toward worry. The future sometimes feels so big, and I forget it's already in your hands. Thank you for offering me peace that doesn't depend on everything working out the way I hoped but on you simply being near. When anxiety creeps in, remind me to breathe deep and trust that you are already working. Help me trade my questions for gratitude and my fear for faith. Amen.

Day 23
The world says the path to success is constant hustle. God says to find rest in Him.

Come to me, all who labor and are heavy laden, and I will give you rest. Take my yoke upon you, and learn from me, for I am gentle and lowly in heart, and you will find rest for your souls. For my yoke is easy, and my burden is light.

- MATTHEW 11:28-30

I don't know many people who aren't busy. Think about it. When was the last time you had a conversation with a girlfriend and she said, "You know, I have been so unhurried lately! My schedule has been so clear. Lately, I have been sitting at home wondering what to do. It's so boring! I wish I had more tasks, meetings, or responsibilities." Yeah, those are conversations that just don't happen.

Instead, when we talk with one another, most of the time, we talk about how hectic our schedules are. We talk about how much time we spend running to the next child's after-school activity. We talk about how busy work has been. We talk about all the chores we have to get done between getting home from work and bedtime. We are all so, so busy.

It's a sign of our times, isn't it? More than that, it's a value our culture passes along. Seriously. Think about it. We get sent so many messages from the world that say the key to success, in multiple areas of life, is to go, go, go! Want to get ahead at work? Hustle. Want to look fit and trim? Make time for the gym. Want to serve your family? Better add meal prep to everything else. Want to make sure the relationships with your husband and kids are thriving? Don't slack off on the home front! Add all of this together, and it makes for an environment ripe for burnout and fatigue.

Our world says that the path to success is to never let up, to hustle, to work hard and fast in every area of your life. But God doesn't value success that way. We should be immensely thankful that this is true.

Some of the most comforting words in Scripture are found in Matthew 11:28-30, where Jesus says, "Come to me, all who labor and are heavy laden, and I will give you rest. Take my yoke upon you, and learn from me, for I am gentle and lowly in heart, and you will find rest for your souls. For my yoke is easy, and my burden is light." Now, Jesus is speaking primarily about salvation and spiritual rest. That's the main message. When people feel burdened by their sin and shame, surrendering in faith to Jesus is the pathway to real soul-rest. But in this verse, and others like it, we see Jesus teaching us that rest is good, right, and valuable. And that He is the source of true rest.

The Bible is clear: There is rest in God. Jeremiah 31:25 says, "For I will satisfy the weary soul, and every languishing soul I will replenish." Exodus 33:14 says, "And he said, 'My presence will go with you, and I will give you rest.'" And one of my favorite verses, "Be still, and know that I am God . . ." (Psalm 46:10).

If I can be transparent, this is an area where I can struggle. I can fall into the trap that says I must hustle all day, or the day is wasted. I thrive on staying busy and productive rather than "sitting around." But often, in my desire to be productive, I neglect time with God and the peace that comes with being still.

Recently, I found myself facing a long string of tasks for the day. I suddenly realized how overwhelming it all felt. I realized that God was telling me to focus on Psalm 46:10. I found myself breathing in deeply and saying to myself, "Be still," then breathing out slowly and saying to myself, "And know that I am God." I did this repeatedly until I felt the truth of what I was saying.

Why do we constantly allow ourselves to fall back into this cycle? Productivity is good. Laziness is not. But at the end of the day, no matter how productive, what truly matters is that we have connected with God and are aware of how He is using us and shaping us. That's real success. The things I accomplish don't matter as much as how I accomplish them. In my rush to be productive, I can often overlook what God is trying to show me and the needs of others.

A soul that finds rest in God is more aware of others' needs and longings, leading to deeper connections. While I sometimes take pride in my "hustle," I'm learning that true joy comes from embracing stillness with God, knowing that everything else will fall into place.

APPLYING GOD'S TRUTH

1. What are the specific areas in your life where you feel the pressure to hustle or constantly be productive?

2. How can you build intentional moments of rest into your day to reconnect with God and experience His peace?

3. Take an intentional break from your busy schedule to go on a nature walk or visit with a family member. If you choose to walk, pay attention to the sights and sounds around you: the leaves, the sun's warmth, or the birds' chirping. During your walk, you can practice the breathing exercises I mentioned earlier. If you're with a loved one, be intentional about focusing solely on the conversation in front of you, rather than thinking about your to-do list.

A PRAYER FOR TODAY

Lord, I'm tired. The pace of this world pushes me to keep running, striving, and achieving. But you invite me to rest. Help me quiet the noise and come to you as I am. Remind me that my worth isn't found in what I do but in who I am in you. Teach me to find peace in your presence and to rest in your goodness. Amen.

Day 24
The world might say that you don't measure up.
God says you are deeply valuable to Him.

I praise you, for I am fearfully and wonderfully made. Wonderful are your works; my soul knows it very well.

- PSALM 139:14

I was blessed to have meaningful relationships with both sets of grand-parents, each remarkable. My paternal grandfather was a decorated war hero and attorney. His wife, my paternal grandmother, lived to be 102 and never lost her sense of style and joy for life. My maternal grandfather was a beloved pastor for over 40 years, and my maternal grandmother served faithfully by his side with unmatched grace and kindness.

I was thinking of my maternal grandfather recently. We called him Grand-daddy, and he was just the most incredible man. He was the most positive person I have ever met; no matter the circumstance, he could always find the silver lining. He loved to laugh. He loved the outdoors. And he was a profoundly spiritual man. Granddaddy was the most loving husband, father, grandfather, and great-grandfather. Even though it has been 15+ years since he entered heaven, he still impacts my life today.

What made him truly special was how he made us feel uniquely valued. With a knowing smile, he'd lean in and say, "You know you're my favorite grandchild, right?" And somehow, in that moment, I believed him. And I'm sure my siblings and cousins felt the same, each walking away thinking we truly were his favorite. Of course, he loved us all equally. But this special little game he played with us sticks out in my mind all these years later because of how valuable it made me feel.

Positivity and encouragement have a way of sticking with us, don't they? Those little compliments, the kind words that lift us up, have a lasting impact on our hearts and minds. They remind us of our worth and our potential. And I think that's because, in a world that sometimes makes us feel small, these words stand out like rays of sunshine breaking through the clouds. They remind us that we are seen and valued.

However, it sometimes feels like the opposite messages find their way to our hearts and minds just as easily. Some of you feel this in your workplace or your community. Unfortunately, some of you feel this in your home. Many of us feel this from a particularly troublesome place: within ourselves. Many of us have a voice inside ourselves that is constantly keeping tabs. "You aren't as pretty as her." "Wow, she is so much smarter than you." "She is so much more successful than you." "No one will look at you like they look at her." The voice of comparison from without and within can be crippling. It can rob us of our joy and make us feel like we don't add up.

We can be eternally thankful that the Bible is full-to-overflowing with assurance that, in God's eyes, you do indeed add up. God values you deeply.

One of my favorite places where we see this is Psalm 139:13–16. This is a beautiful expression of God's tremendous value for us. The picture that this passage paints is of a God who chose you. God didn't literally put us together in our mother's womb. We know a little more about anatomy and reproduction than David did! But David is accurately showing that God not only created you, but that you were created with His knowledge. You didn't happen by accident. You didn't sneak in under the radar. You have breath and life because God wanted you to. It doesn't stop there.

Jesus Himself shows us the depth of the value God places on us. In Matthew 10:29–31, He says, "Are not two sparrows sold for a penny? And not one of them will fall to the ground apart from your Father. But even the hairs of your head are all numbered. Fear not, therefore; you are of more value than many sparrows." In Jesus' time, a sparrow was about as small and insignificant an animal as there was. And Jesus is saying here that God knows the fate of every sparrow that has ever lived. If that's true about sparrows, how much more true is it about us?

God knows you. He values you. He loves you. There can be no fuller expression of this than the Gospel itself. "For God so loved the world, that he gave his only Son, that whoever believes in him should not perish but have eternal life" (John 3:16). If God's sending of His beloved Son to die in your place so that you may have life isn't an expression of your value, then I don't know what is.

What made my Granddaddy's pronouncements that we were his favorite so meaningful wasn't just the words he said, but the way he made us feel: cherished, valued, and loved. In the same way, God looks at us and feels that even more strongly than we could ever imagine. When He made you, He saw you and loved you! He thinks you are amazing and gives you gifts for His glory and your good.

Friend, you are valued by the Creator God, the eternal, perfect, righteous Father. And nothing the world can say against you can change that.

APPLYING GOD'S TRUTH

1. Choose someone who may need a reminder that they are cherished and valued. It could be a family member, friend, or even a stranger. Write them a heartfelt note, send a text, or do something special to show them that they matter.

2. Do you ever struggle with feelings of inadequacy or comparison? How does Psalm 139:14 remind you of the deep value God has placed on your life?

3. Think about the voices you listen to, whether from others or within yourself. Are they affirming your worth in Christ or tearing you down? How can you begin replacing lies with God's truth?

4. Jesus said God knows every sparrow and values us even more (Matthew 10:29–31). How does this change the way you see yourself and others? How can you live more fully in that truth?

A PRAYER FOR TODAY

Father, thank you for creating me with intention and love, for seeing me as valuable even when I struggle to believe it. Please help me to silence the lies of comparison and rest in the truth that I am fearfully and wonderfully made. Let me reflect your love by affirming the worth of those around me, just as you have affirmed mine. Amen.

Day 25
The world says it's all on you.
God says that His strength will carry you.

But he said to me, "My grace is sufficient for you, for my power is made perfect in weakness." Therefore I will boast all the more gladly of my weaknesses, so that the power of Christ may rest upon me. For the sake of Christ, then, I am content with weaknesses, insults, hardships, persecutions, and calamities. For when I am weak, then I am strong.

- 2 CORINTHIANS 12:9–10

I constantly find myself blown away by just how awesome the women I encounter each day are. Whether on social media, in news articles, or in person, it seems like all around us, women are doing so many amazing things. They are running small business side-hustles (some of which have become main hustles!). They are business leaders, creators, writers, actors, moms, preachers, teachers, and so on, and they are fantastic. Some of them are my friends, and some are people I'll never meet. But I am in awe of the talent and skill level of so many women I encounter each day.

It's easy to celebrate the accomplishments of others, and they deserve it. But here's the thing: many of us find ourselves in a quiet struggle when we compare our journey to theirs. When we measure ourselves against high achievers, it's easy to feel like we don't quite measure up. Our lives might be good, but maybe not as great as we see in those recognized on social media and elsewhere. We start thinking, "They've got the skills, the talent, the abilities. And me? Not so much."

The world says if we're talented, we'll go places. If we're strong enough, we can conquer the world. But if not? Well, maybe life will still be nice, but it won't be like theirs (whoever they are).

Friend, take comfort in this: that's not how God works. He doesn't measure us by our abilities or our talent. Instead, He sees the heart and the purpose He's placed in each one of us. Our worth isn't found in the comparison game, but in the unique way God has called us to live.

Make sure you read 2 Corinthians 12:9–10 because some powerful truth is being dropped here. This is, of course, the Apostle Paul writing a letter to the church in Corinth, telling them a wild story. Basically, he was so incredible at preaching, teaching, and sharing the Gospel that God was worried Paul might become conceited. (These are Paul's words, not mine!) So, to humble him, God sent what Paul called a "thorn in his flesh." There have been plenty of people over the centuries with different opinions of what this thorn in the flesh was. Paul didn't come out and say it, so we don't know. But we know that it was something unpleasant designed to get Paul's attention.

Paul asked God to take away this thorn. Paul says that he begged God, and God didn't answer his prayer as Paul wanted. Instead, we get the response you just read. I imagine 2 Corinthians 12:9–10 is God saying to Paul, "You're great at what you do! You're so gifted and so skilled. But remember, I am the one who has made you and planned out your path. I am the one who goes before you. I am your source of strength, not you. Trust in me, not in your abilities." It sure seems like this changed everything for Paul! Look at his response: "Therefore I will boast all the more gladly of my weaknesses, so that the power of Christ may rest upon me" (2 Corinthians 12:9).

Friend, in God's Kingdom, we are strongest when we own our weaknesses. We must accept our limitations and look to God as the source of all our strength. When we are weak, we are strong in Christ.

I mentioned earlier that I had back surgery in 2021 after an injury during a HIIT workout. I write and speak about this a lot because it was truly a dark period in my life. It was pretty bad, but God taught me so much. The road to recovery was, at times, excruciating and truly testing. Part of the physical therapy was simply walking laps around my kitchen for 10 minutes. That was the goal. And guess what? It was tough. It seems so easy to mention now, but it was excruciating when I was doing it. What I wanted to do was stay in bed.

To get through these laps, I'd turn up worship music and sing loudly while walking. (A sight to see, I know!) One song specifically was "You Know My Name" by CeCe Winans. I would play this song repeatedly, reminding me of God's eye on me. I was not forgotten. He saw me. And in those moments, He was my strength. My flesh wanted to give up, but I would turn that song on and hear that wonderful reminder: He knows my name. He is my strength. I am weak, but He is strong. He sees me, He hears my cries, He knows my pain.

Looking back, I felt so close to God during that time. I wouldn't choose to go back through that pain, but I am here to say that He truly was sufficient in my weakness. Over time, God healed me, but He left me with a wonderful lesson: When God is our source of strength, there is nothing He wants for us that we can't achieve.

The world says you will only go as far as your strength will carry you. God says, My strength, and my strength alone, will carry you and accomplish my plan for you. Trust in this truth: God is your source of strength! Take a deep breath and lean into Him today by letting go.

APPLYING GOD'S TRUTH

1. Have you ever felt inadequate when comparing yourself to others' achievements? How does 2 Corinthians 12:9–10 shift your perspective on where true strength comes from?

2. What weaknesses or struggles have led you to rely more on God? How have you seen His strength carry you through?

3. When you face challenges, do you instinctively try to push through in your own strength, or do you pause to seek God's help? How can you develop a habit of leaning on His power daily?

4. Paul embraced his weakness so that God's strength could be made known. What would it look like to stop striving in your own effort and rest in God's sufficiency instead?

A PRAYER FOR TODAY

Father, thank you for reminding me that my strength is not found in my abilities but in your power at work within me. When I feel weak, let me lean on you, knowing your grace is always enough. Teach me to trust in your strength rather than my own, and help me to rest in the confidence that you are always with me. Amen.

Day 26
The world says chaos is normal.
God says that peace is found in Him.

Do not be anxious about anything, but in everything by prayer and supplication with thanksgiving let your requests be made known to God. And the peace of God, which surpasses all understanding, will guard your hearts and your minds in Christ Jesus.

- PHILIPPIANS 4:6–7

I know it's hard to escape the chaos of the world, right? A quick scroll through social media or a glance at the news, and it's all around us. But it's not just the big things; sometimes, everyday stressors, like balancing family, work, and life, add up. If we're not careful, we can start to believe that this constant hustle and rush is just how life must be. But here's the good news: it doesn't have to be like this.

God speaks directly to this and provides us with a wonderful alternative. God says, "The world is chaotic sometimes, but I am a God of peace. I will give you peace during chaos." For some of us, this is the most comforting promise there is.

Take a moment and read Philippians 4:6–7. We know Paul wrote the letter to the Philippians. He would have written it around 30 years after Jesus' death and resurrection. But the most important thing to remember is that Paul is writing this from prison. There is some debate about when he wrote the letter and where exactly he was imprisoned, but the fact is that Paul's life had been turned upside down. He had been arrested because of his commitment to the Gospel and put in jail. He would eventually be murdered for his faith.

In 2024, our family had the incredible opportunity to visit Rome, and let me tell you, what an adventure! We explored several historical sites, including the ruins of places where Paul might have been imprisoned. And, as you can imagine, these were not 5-star accommodations. But as I sat there, reflecting on Paul's time in prison, I was struck by something so powerful. In the middle of his chaos and hardship, Paul wasn't filled with anxiety. Instead, he took his concerns and worries to God through prayer.

And guess what? God gave him peace. And that same peace is available to us today. Even though it's been 2,000 years, Paul's advice to the Philippians still applies perfectly to us. Isn't that just amazing?

As I've mentioned in the introduction, before I left marriage and family therapy to run my lifestyle brand, one of the most effective tools I used with my clients was helping them reframe their thoughts about stressful situations. As a reminder, reframing is simply taking a negative thought and turning it into something more positive. For example, if someone said, "My husband always rushes out the door for church, and it stresses me out," a reframe would be, "Maybe he's rushing because being on time is important to him, and I can respect that."

This simple concept is just as powerful when life feels overwhelming. I've tried reframing my thoughts in those moments when the house needs tidying up, the sink is full of dishes, laundry's waiting to be folded, and homework still needs to be done. Instead of feeling frazzled, I remind myself, "In a couple of hours, this feeling will have passed. The house will look different, and things will be more settled." That shift in perspective helps bring peace in those moments.

But the truth that always grounds me is this: God promises us peace amid the chaos. No matter what's happening around us, He's there, offering calm and comfort when we need it most.

God is our peace, all the time. Maybe today, you can try reframing how you view the chaos around you. God is the peace that keeps our feet on solid ground when the world wants to pull us in a million different directions. It's such a lovely thought, isn't it?

Chaos doesn't get the last word. God does. And His Word speaks peace to chaos.

APPLYING GOD'S TRUTH

1. What are some areas in your life where you feel overwhelmed by chaos or stress? How might intentionally turning to God in prayer, as Philippians 4:6–7 encourages, bring you peace?

2. Paul found peace amid imprisonment. What does that teach you about the kind of peace God offers? How does His peace differ from the temporary relief the world provides?

3. Think about a recent stressful situation. How could you "reframe" your thoughts to see God's presence in it rather than being consumed by anxiety?

4. What practical step can you take today to slow down, refocus, and rest in the peace that God freely gives?

A PRAYER FOR TODAY

Father, when the world feels chaotic and overwhelming, remind me that you are my peace. Help me to release my anxieties to you in prayer, trusting that your presence is greater than my circumstances. Teach me to rest in the stillness of your promises, knowing that you are always in control. Amen.

Day 27
The world says love is conditional.
God says that His love is unconditional.

But God, being rich in mercy, because of the great love with which he loved us, even when we were dead in our trespasses, made us alive together with Christ—by grace you have been saved.

- EPHESIANS 2:4-5

God is love! He is good, He is for you, and He is with you. You may know this love already, but oftentimes, we have to remind ourselves of it because it's so opposite to what we see in front of us. This love changes everything about who we are and how we view ourselves.

What is the one area of your life where you struggle with feeling "enough"?

From one friend to another, I see you sitting there, wondering if you're doing a good enough job taking care of those around you. I see you wondering if you were "pretty" enough for the friends you had lunch with today. I see you worrying about whether you showed your children enough attention today. I see you questioning whether you were productive enough today. Or if anyone even noticed your work.

There are areas in our lives where we hold ourselves to an impossible standard. I have them, and I am guessing you do too.

We've been told that if we can just be efficient enough, put together enough, or do enough work, then we will be seen, loved, and cherished. This kind of love is transactional.

Unfortunately, this message is so intertwined with how we, as mothers, daughters, wives, or friends, view ourselves at times. Did we perform well enough to earn the love and appreciation of those around us?

Our knowledge makes us more respected, so we must learn more. Our physical shape makes us more admired, so we had better work out harder. Our career achievements make us valued, so we achieve. I know the world sends these messages to women because I have heard them myself, time and time again.

Read Ephesians 2:1–10. This is one of the many places in the Bible where we see the Gospel fleshed out in all its beauty. In verses 1–3, the Apostle Paul shows us that apart from a relationship with Jesus, we're in rebellion against God. This rebellion is sin, and it has a specific outcome. Sin causes separation from God, and separation from God is spiritual death.

But look back to verse 1 for that beautiful phrase, "in which you once walked." Through faith in Jesus, what was once true for us isn't true any longer! God makes a way back to a relationship with us, His fallen children, through the life, death, and resurrection of His Son, Jesus. That's amazing grace! And our focus today is on verses 4–5 and God's unconditional love for us, which is the opposite of the transactional love described above.

When we come to God and believe in the Good News of the Gospel, we aren't bringing our best selves; we're spiritually dead and separated by our sins. But God, out of His perfect and unconditional love, offers us forgiveness and makes us new.

God's love for you was there even when you were separated from Him. Can you even imagine how perfectly unconditional God's love for you is now that He sees you through the lens of His Son's sacrifice for you?

Here's the powerful truth: keeping up with the world's performance- or transaction-based love makes us weary and sets a standard for ourselves we'll never meet. But Jesus' love is life-giving, hope-filled, tender, all-encompassing, and will never change. You can't earn it or do enough things for it, and yet it is there for you always.

I pray you never grow weary of hearing how much God loves us. He loves you so much!

APPLYING GOD'S TRUTH

1. How often do you find yourself trying to earn love and approval through your actions and achievements? Take a moment to write down ways in which you have sought validation from others this week.

2. How does knowing that God's love is unconditional change your perspective on your worth and value?

3. What would it look like to live, one day, fully resting in God's love instead of striving for the world's approval?

A PRAYER FOR TODAY

Dear Father, I'm tired of trying to be enough. Thank you for loving me with a love that doesn't depend on my performance or perfection. Help me believe, deep in my soul, that your grace is real and your love is mine, always. Teach me to rest in that truth today, and to live from a place of being already cherished, not endlessly striving to be.
Amen.

Day 28
The world says work is a grind.
God says there is purpose in our work.

Whatever you do, work heartily, as for the Lord and not for men, knowing that from the Lord you will receive the inheritance as your reward. You are serving the Lord Christ. For the wrongdoer will be paid back for the wrong he has done, and there is no partiality.

- COLOSSIANS 3:23–25

I remember when my daughters were first old enough to get after-school jobs. Andy and I raised our children with a strong work ethic. They wanted to work to fill their spare time and earn a little bit of extra pocket money. I remember being their age and working after-school jobs. There was something so grown-up about it.

Our oldest daughters are only a grade apart, and they ended up getting jobs at the same place. This was a new retail store with a first-time owner, and the first few days were enjoyable. Everyone liked them. There was a novelty to the "sisters." Work was new, fresh, and fun. But after a week or so, that story changed slightly.

At first, it was all excitement with fun stories, great coworkers, and small wins. But over time, the conversations started to shift. Tough managers, growing pains, and office drama weren't all bad, but the shine had worn off, and reality had settled in.

Of course, this opened the door for many heart-to-heart conversations about having a godly attitude, staying committed, and all those little life lessons that shape us. But at the end of the day, I just wanted them to see that this is simply how the world works sometimes. One day, amid another round of them talking about things being tough at work, my husband smiled and said something I've heard him say more times than I can count: "There's a reason they have to pay you to do it." And, of course, there's so much truth in that.

Let's be real: work can sometimes feel like a grind for many of us. Whether it's a career, running a business, or managing a busy home, even the most rewarding jobs can have moments where the sparkle fades. It's easy to fall into the mindset that work is just a never-ending cycle. Get through the day, check things off, and then start again. But what if we chose to look at it differently? What if we saw our work as a meaningful part of our journey, a place where we get to make a difference, no matter how small it may seem in the moment?

Take a moment and read Colossians 3:23–24. Paul didn't start the church in Colossae like he did so many others. It probably began during Paul's ministry in Ephesus when a guy named Epaphras heard the Gospel, and after believing, returned home and shared what had happened to him. Others heard and believed. At some point, Epaphras joined Paul and probably reported that the church was experiencing some issues. In response, Paul writes the letter to address the problems and encourage the Colossians. The same thing Paul did for the Colossians, he does for us: he helps us see how God's Word confronts the world's opinions.

In Colossians 3:23–24, Paul reminds us that our work is not just a never-ending cycle to endure, but an opportunity to glorify God. Whether we work from home, at an office, or in a caregiving role, our attitude makes all the difference. Paul encourages us to work as though we serve God, not just our current boss. Imagine the change in perspective if we saw our tasks as being done for Him instead of just for a paycheck.

I can personally relate to this lesson. Working at a children's hospital in the cardiac intensive care unit was one of my life's most challenging and rewarding seasons. I worked with people I deeply respected, but the tension from different values and beliefs made the environment tough. It was draining. Some days, I left work with tears in my eyes, leaning on praise music to help me press on. Despite the challenges, I knew God had called me to that job. I had to dig deep and find joy amid the struggle. And I did, until He called me elsewhere.

Work has purpose, whether it's your dream job or one that feels like a grind. God gave Adam work in the Garden of Eden to nurture and care for it (Genesis 2:15), showing that work is part of His design. Even in the hardest days, remember that we work not just for the world but for something greater. Every task is an opportunity to honor God. And that, my sweet friend, is a blessing.

APPLYING GOD'S TRUTH

1. How does Colossians 3:23–25 challenge or encourage your current view of work?

2. Can you think of a time when a demanding job or task became meaningful because you approached it as service to God? What changed in your heart or attitude?

3. What would it look like for you to work "for the Lord and not for men" in your current season, whether it's in a career, at home, or in ministry?

A PRAYER FOR TODAY

Father, thank you for giving meaning to our work. Even when it feels mundane or heavy, remind us that we ultimately serve you. Help us to work with joy, diligence, and a heart set on honoring you in every task. Teach us to see our responsibilities not as burdens, but as places of purpose where your presence meets our effort. May our labor reflect our love for you. In Jesus' name, Amen.

Day 29
The world says there is no truth.
God says that His Word is true.

All Scripture is breathed out by God and profitable for teaching, for reproof, for correction, and for training in righteousness, that the man of God may be complete, equipped for every good work.

- 2 TIMOTHY 3:16-17

Over the years, Andy and I have had conversations with our children that go like this: "If you see or hear anything from friends—at school, church, or wherever—that you are confused about or have a feeling is not right, come talk to us about it. We will talk through it together and figure out what it is all about." We let them know that we will listen and tell them the truth about whatever they have heard or seen.

If you have children, I'm sure you may have said something similar. As parents, we want to be the source where they can find truth and not the world. Truth is comforting for children, especially when they are first being exposed to the broader world. Confusion, uncertainty, and even harm can result from hearing and believing half-truths and outright lies they learn from the world around them. The promise that they can come to us and hear the truth relieves them of the anxiety and confusion that untruths cause.

Isn't it the same with us? The world around us loves to say that there is no source of absolute or authoritative truth. What phrases do you hear around you? "Well, my truth is . . ." Or "Well, that's your truth, but that's not my truth." Sometimes, when I hear people saying this, I wonder if we all realize how nonsensical this sounds! Truth is only truth if it is universally true. If your truth is different than my truth, is it truth at all?

Into this cultural reality, the "capital-t" truth of God's Word shines through. God is true. God is truthful. And God's Word, the Bible, is 100% true. It is reliable. It is unchanging. It is as authentic and unfailing today as it was when the Spirit inspired its authors to write it thousands of years ago. Friend, it is essential to our Christian lives that we remember this.

Read 2 Timothy 3:16–17. Paul wrote 1st and 2nd Timothy to encourage and guide Timothy, a young pastor in Ephesus. Paul had met Timothy on his missionary journeys, mentored him, and even called him his "spiritual son."

As Timothy led the church, he faced challenges, including false teachers spreading false teaching. In verses 16–17, Paul reminds him that Scripture is God's truth, equipping us to stand firm in faith. His words weren't just for Timothy; they're for us today.

God's Word is our foundation. It always shapes, corrects, and equips us to live faithfully. Are you anchored in it?

The Bible is "God-breathed." Isn't that a powerful image? (Paul made up the Greek word he used here!) We know that human beings wrote the actual words we know as our Bible, but God, through His Spirit, inspired those words. The same Spirit that breathed life into Adam in Genesis 2:7 breathed the words of the Bible into existence. The Bible is true because He is truth. We can trust that it is everything God wanted us to know about life and faith.

Friend, don't we still struggle at times, filling our heads and hearts with untruths? Have you considered what one-liners you may be telling yourself repeatedly today? We see, hear, and even feel untruths all around us. Today, I urge you to open God's Word, the only source of unchanging truth.

It has been said that the Bible is a mirror (the only way we truly see ourselves) and a window (the only true way to see the world). Our calling, as Christians, is to grow a vibrant, daily relationship with God, and what better way than through the Bible, God's true words to us.

APPLYING GOD'S TRUTH

1. What cultural "truths" have you encountered that conflict with God's Word? How have they influenced your thinking, and how can you intentionally filter what you take in through the lens of Scripture?

2. When you face uncertainty or doubt, do you instinctively turn to God's Word for guidance or seek answers elsewhere? How can you develop a deeper trust in Scripture as your source of truth?

3. What practical steps can you take to anchor yourself daily in God's truth through reading, memorization, or intentional reflection? How might this impact your ability to stand firm against the shifting messages of the world?

A PRAYER FOR TODAY

Father, in a world filled with uncertainty and confusion, help me to stand firm on your unchanging truth. Guard my heart and mind from the world's lies and draw me deeper into your Word so that I may know and trust you more. May your Spirit guide me to walk in wisdom, confidence, and faith, always anchored in the truth of who you are. Amen.

Day 30
The world may call you a mess.
God says that you're a beautiful work in progress.

And I am sure of this, that He who began a good work in you will bring it to completion at the day of Jesus Christ.

These days, most of my working day is spent dreaming up content, building marketing campaigns, and thinking through the many pieces that go into running a business. But for over a decade, my workdays looked very different.

As I have mentioned, for nearly 13 years, I began each day helping people navigate through some of the most painful and difficult seasons of their lives. As a Marriage and Family Therapist, I had the privilege of walking alongside people in their most vulnerable moments. I worked in private practice. I spent time on the psychiatric unit of a large hospital. I served as a grief counselor for families experiencing heartbreaking loss; parents who had lost children and children who had lost parents. I even worked on a cardiac care team evaluating children waiting for heart transplants.

It was heavy work. Some days, the sorrow I encountered felt overwhelming. But even on the hardest days, what kept me going was this: witnessing healing. I watched people who had every reason to give up begin rebuilding their lives. I saw the beauty of resilience in action. I saw couples mend broken marriages. I saw individuals face down anxiety and depression, and begin to live life again. I saw those who had been deeply hurt by others walk forward in forgiveness and find peace. And every single time, I was reminded of the profound truth that there is always hope.

Hope that where you are now isn't where you'll stay.

Hope that God isn't done writing your story.

But I know that kind of hope can sometimes be forgotten. We're quick to believe the world's message that says, "You're a mess." We replay our past mistakes and let them name us. We compare our lives to others and feel like we'll never measure up. We focus on the parts of ourselves we wish were different and think, "This is just how I'll always be." But hear this, sweet friend:

You are not a screw-up.

And you are not behind.

You are a beautiful work in progress.

God is not finished with you. If you're still breathing, He's still moving. Philippians 1:6 reminds us, "He who began a good work in you will bring it to completion." That means your story isn't over. It's still unfolding. There is purpose in the progress, even in the parts that feel slow or unseen.

First and foremost, Paul is speaking about our sanctification in that verse, the great picture of God's ongoing, loving work in our lives. The beauty of sanctification is that God, through the power of His Spirit, shapes us to become more like Jesus. It's not overnight. It's not always pretty. But it is holy and beautiful. It's proof that God doesn't leave us where He found us. And that truth gives us so much hope.

I think of Paul again in 2 Corinthians 4:16, reminding his readers and himself not to give up: "So we do not lose heart. Though our outer self is wasting away, our inner self is being renewed day by day." Paul's body was tired, and his circumstances were hard. But inwardly, God was still doing a work. God hadn't let go. And He hasn't let go of you, either.

You may not be where you want to be yet. You may still be healing, growing, and becoming. But even now, God is shaping you lovingly and faithfully into the person He created you to be.

So today, take a deep breath. Your past doesn't define you, and your mistakes don't limit God. Your weaknesses? They're simply invitations for His strength to shine. Keep going, friend.

APPLYING GOD'S TRUTH

1. Where have you seen evidence, big or small, that God is growing or changing something in your life recently? Reflect on even the most minor shifts in your thinking, habits, or responses and thank God for His work in you.

2. What lies from the world (or your inner critic) have you believed about your identity, and how do they contrast with what God says about you? Use Scripture to counter those lies and remind yourself of the truth.

3. Is there an area of your life where you feel "unfinished" or discouraged? How might Philippians 1:6 reshape how you view that area in light of God's ongoing faithfulness?

A PRAYER FOR TODAY

Father, thank you for never giving up on me. In a world that calls out my flaws, you gently remind me that I am your beloved work in progress. Help me to trust that the transformation you've begun in me will not be abandoned. Give me eyes to see growth where I feel stuck, and faith to believe that you are constantly shaping me into someone more like Jesus. Amen.

Day 31
The world loves instant gratification.
God invites us to trust His perfect timing.

Better is the end of a thing than its beginning, and the patient in spirit is better than the proud in spirit.

- ECCLESIASTES 7:8

I was so excited the first time we visited Disney World with our children because they had just launched the Fast Pass, allowing you to circumvent long lines and walk up to the most popular rides. The process has changed so much since then, but when Fast Pass was first introduced, it was beautifully simple. It lowered your wait time in lines, allowing you to ride more attractions quickly and move on to the next thing. It had a lot of perks: less time in the hot sun, happier children, and more rides completed throughout the day. The first couple of times we took our kids to Disney, we utilized them to maximum effect.

There are a lot of things in our lives that work like that, right? Do you want to lose weight? These days, you can do it faster with prescription medication. How about shopping? No more ordering something and waiting 5–10 business days. Some items on Amazon are available for same-day delivery. Drive-throughs were an awesome invention in the 50s. But now meal delivery services have made fast food even more convenient.

Think of the last time you had to wait longer than you expected in a drive-through. What was your attitude? How did it affect your mood? As a culture, we don't really value waiting. Many people say that time is their most valuable commodity—instant rice, instant coffee, instant financing, etc. We will do anything to save or maximize our time.

It's not just adults who feel this way. When your child was hungry as a toddler, they likely didn't sit and wait peacefully. They probably started crying or acting up to let you know they wanted food. Maybe some of your teenagers still act the same way. (Ha!)

The only issue is that waiting is often the best way to learn patience. And whether you value patience as a quality or not, God certainly does. It's a fruit of the Spirit, after all. And yet, patience is seemingly a fleeting virtue in our world, even among Christians.

Even if you know them by heart, take another look at the fruit of the Spirit in Galatians 5:22. Here, the Holy Spirit, working through Paul to put down these mighty words, teaches us a fundamental truth: these virtues that we see listed here are only alive and active in us because the Spirit is alive and active in us.

However, the fruit of the Spirit, no matter what we teach young children, isn't like the fruit on a tree. It's not that kind of fruit that Paul is talking about. The best way to understand the "fruit" Paul is talking about is to think of "fruit" as the results. Have you heard the saying, "the fruit of your labor"? That's what Paul means here. Just like the fruit (results) of your work is a paycheck, a beautiful flower garden, or a nice apple pie, the fruit (results) of the work of the Spirit in us is virtue!

I love because the Spirit is in me and compels me to love. I have joy because the Spirit is in me, and He makes me joyful (which is the only way to have joy in the midst of trials). I am not patient because I have strong willpower or have mastered the art of meditative breathing. I am patient because God's Spirit dwells within me and works patience in and out through me.

So, yes, patience is a virtue, and if you've been around patient people, they are often peaceful. For Christians, both aspects of our character come from the Holy Spirit within us. The result of God's work in us is that the constant need for instant gratification, which can lead to chaos, oversaturation, and ultimately emptiness, is often absent. And if it is present in your life, it's a good sign that there is still work to be done in surrendering control of your emotions to God.

In Ecclesiastes 7:8, Solomon writes, "Better is the end of a thing than its beginning, and the patient in spirit is better than the proud in spirit." We don't often think of pride and patience as opposites, or even as related at all. And yet, the proud person tries to handle this world and its demands on their own. It's a losing battle. For the Christian, humility leads to patience. When we surrender ourselves to God and to the leading of His Spirit, He works within our hearts to make us more patient. It's a promise. He will do it. We must be open to it.

When we exhibit patience, we're showing God to those around us. Think about a time when someone extended patience to you. Didn't it leave you feeling understood and even loved?

APPLYING GOD'S TRUTH

Today, instead of discussion questions, let's get active. Choose one (or all) of these three ways to show patience to others today:

1. **Listen Actively and Without Interruptions**
   When someone is speaking to you, make a conscious effort to listen without interrupting. This not only shows respect but also demonstrates patience. Give them your full attention, nod, and respond thoughtfully, even if you're in a hurry.

2. **Be Patient in Traffic or Long Lines**
   Whether you're stuck in traffic or waiting in a long line, use the time to practice patience. Instead of getting frustrated, take a few deep breaths, say a prayer, or listen to a worship song. Show kindness to those around you by remaining calm and composed.

3. **Respond with Grace**
   When someone makes a mistake or things don't go as planned, respond with grace instead of frustration. Offer encouragement and support instead of criticism. Recognize that everyone has off days, and showing patience can be a powerful testimony of God's love and grace.

A PRAYER FOR TODAY

Lord, help me trust your timing even when I feel impatient or restless.
Teach me to wait well, knowing you are never late and always good.
Grow in me a Spirit-led patience that reflects your grace to those
around me. I surrender my need for control and choose to rest in you.
Amen.

ABOUT THE AUTHOR

Brendt Blanks (pronounced "Brent"—the "d" is silent) is the founder of She Gave It A Go, a space where faith, family, and home decorating come together. A passionate Christ-follower, she sees life through the lens of the Gospel and embraces the full life Jesus promises in John 10:10.

Married since 2000, Brendt and her husband, Andy, have four wonderful children. Before launching She Gave It A Go, she worked as a licensed Marriage and Family Therapist, dedicating her career to helping others thrive. Family remains at the heart of everything she does, and she loves encouraging women to create homes filled with love and purpose.

Brendt's passion for decorating led her to create She Gave It A Go, where she shares home inspiration, DIY projects, decorating tips, and more. Whether offering styling ideas or faith-filled encouragement, her goal is to help others find joy in making their spaces beautiful and meaningful.

Through She Gave It A Go, Brendt connects with a community that shares her love for faith, family, and home, offering inspiration and encouragement every step of the way.

Equipping the Church to know God
through His Word.

ironhillpress.com   800.307.9366